The Ultimate
Internal Medicine Training
Application Guide

Previous Editions: 2019, 2018

ISBN 978-1-912557-58-5

Published by *RAR Medical Services Limited*
www.oxbridgemedicalsociety.com

The Ultimate
Internal Medicine Training
Application Guide

Dr Charles Earnshaw

Dr Rohan Agarwal

Edited by Dr Ranjna Garg

About the Authors

Charles is as an **Academic Clinical Fellow** in Dermatology, and is funded by the National Institute for Health Research. He has a strong interest in medical education, and taught Pathology to dozens of undergraduates whilst a student at Gonville and Caius College, Cambridge. He has successfully interviewed for several competitive positions and scholarships, and has taught interview techniques to many students during his career to date.

Charles has a desire to run his own molecular biology research laboratory. He has published in the fields of oncology and immunology, and is working towards his PhD Fellowship Application. He enjoys mountaineering and photography.

Rohan is the **Director of Operations** at *UniAdmissions* and is responsible for its technical and commercial arms. He graduated from Gonville and Caius College, Cambridge and is a fully qualified doctor. Over the last five years, he has tutored hundreds of successful Oxbridge and Medical applicants. He has also authored ten books on admissions tests and interviews.

Rohan has taught physiology to undergraduates and interviewed medical school applicants for Cambridge. He has published research on bone physiology and writes education articles for the Independent and Huffington Post. In his spare time, Rohan enjoys playing the piano and table tennis.

About the Editor

Ranjna is as a **Consultant Physician** at the Royal Free Trust London NHS Foundation Trust. Over the last decade, she has taught hundreds of junior doctors and prepared them through postgraduate examinations and job interviews. She enjoys helping students with their medical school preparation and has interviewed for London medical schools as well.

She has done significant research on the use of high strength insulin for patients with severe insulin resistance. In her spare time, she enjoys photography and running.

Foreword

Internal Medicine Stage 1 (IM) is an exciting and diverse training programme. It is the foundation for a career in any medical specialty – from Gastroenterology to Genetics, Neurology to Nephrology – and therefore a large range of doctors from different backgrounds apply for competitive entry each year.

Progression to Specialist Registrar training within any these broad medical specialties is dependent on successful completion of IM. This book aims to provide a standardised approach to the application process and interview that aims to help a wide variety of candidates be successful with their application.

The 2019 entry is the first year that IM replaces Core Medical Training. Understandably, this fact will generate some concern and uncertainty, particularly amongst the initial group of applicants, but we will cover both the main changes brought about by IM, and, importantly, the main aspects that will remain the same. This should remove many of the fears that you might have about this exciting and new training programme.

We realise that for some applicants, this may be the first medical interview they have since they applied for medical school. This brings with it unique challenges – the breadth and depth of knowledge and experience gained throughout medical school and in the Foundation Programme is available to be drawn upon in the application, and tested at the interview. The strategies presented throughout this book enable you to maximise your performance in both components.

Fundamentally, we believe job interviews are something that you should look forward to. They are an opportunity to enthusiastically explain why you want to do a job that you have specifically chosen to apply to. They are an opportunity to talk about yourself and the experiences that have brought you to the interview. They allow you to meet future colleagues and mentors.

We hope this book will increase your anticipation of IM as a training programme, and remove some of the fears you may have associated with the IM application and interview. We are confident that you will have a much stronger idea of what to expect throughout the application process, and that this will translate into a much more enjoyable experience at the interview.

Good luck!

Dr Charles Earnshaw & Dr Rohan Agarwal

HOW TO USE THIS BOOK

This book is designed to be a comprehensive guide to the full application process for Internal Medicine Stage 1. Therefore, it covers preparation prior to completing the online application, through to a detailed discussion regarding what to expect at the interview. As such, early engagement with this book is likely to prove most successful during your application process.

We would recommend reading through the chapters about the person specification and the online application at least a month prior to completing the application, if not earlier. This allows you to plan your application with plenty of time to spare, and provides time for you to follow some of our tips that may enable you to increase the overall score of your application. It also gives you plenty of time to prepare your portfolio prior to the interview, as you will learn exactly what you need to include in your portfolio.

Reading through the chapters regarding the interview a couple of times is always a good idea – once to discover what the interview will be like, and potentially remove some of your fears – and once closer to the interview itself to refresh what the day will be like and what knowledge you need to brush up on. Reading these chapters early is also advisable as you may pick up important tips that you need time to implement effectively – such as realising the importance of mock interviews, which can take time to organise.

This book is not designed to tell you what your application and interview style must be like – instead, it provides information and advice based around previous highly successful applications, and lessons that those applicants learned during the process. Your application must always remain true to you as an individual, and the book aims to give these tips in a way that complements rather than dictates your application. Used in this way, the book should maximise your chances of success in the application. We hope you enjoy your experience using it.

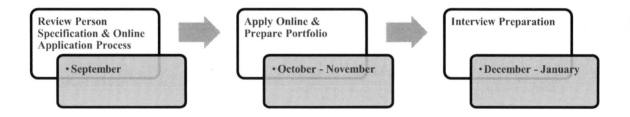

Review Person Specification & Online Application Process		Apply Online & Prepare Portfolio		Interview Preparation
• September	→	• October - November	→	• December - January

INTERNAL MEDICINE STAGE 1

The Shape of Training reforms are introducing the most significant changes to postgraduate medical training in many years. There are several reasons driving this, but arguably the most important one is the need to adapt the medical profession to be able to deal with the ageing and increasingly co-morbid population.

Broadly speaking, Core Medical Training (CMT) is being replaced by a new 'Internal Medicine Stage 1' (IM) programme. This will be either two or three years long, depending on which medical specialty the applicant wishes to apply for: certain specialties will be able to recruit applicants directly from the second year of IM (IM2), whereas others will take applicants only following completion of the full three year training pathway. The programme places an emphasis on training the future medical consultants of the NHS through a variety of inpatient and outpatient experiences, and this aim is reflected in the application process.

We will cover the main changes brought about in IM, and discuss how this changes when you will apply to different specialties. We will not cover the entire curriculum or provide in depth discussion of how Shape of Training will affect registrar training: our aim is prepare you further for your Internal Medicine Stage 1 application and interview.

The IM Job Remains Similar to CMT

The new Internal Medicine Stage 1 will remain broadly similar to Core Medical Training, with the same end goal of training the future consultants of the NHS. As is currently the situation, there will be significant exposure to the acute medical on call rota, with responsibilities ranging from providing ward cover to coordinating acute medical admissions from the Accident and Emergency department and local General Practitioners.

As was the case throughout the Foundation Programme, the online portfolio plays an important role in the successful completion of IM. Once again, reflection and supervised learning events, such as case-based discussions, provide an important structure to showing evidence that the trainee is ready to officially complete IM.

Throughout the programme there is an important emphasis on scheduled teaching. A variety of local and deanery-wide sessions are provided on medical topics and practical techniques. Trainees are also expected to engage with a Quality Improvement project in each year of the programme, and so expect this to be a possible topic for discussion at interview.

In addition, trainees are expected to gain a full membership of the Royal College of Physicians during the programme. This currently consists of the written exams, Part I and Part II, and the practical PACES examination. Once the trainee has full MRCP(UK) status, they are able to commence specialty training: therefore, completion of the portfolio requirements, as well as the full MRCP(UK), are steps needed for successful completion of IM.

Specialty Training: Group 1 vs. Group 2 Specialties

Following completion of the second and third year of IM, the trainee will have the opportunity to enter Specialty Training. These specialties are divided into two groups: Group 1 and Group 2. These two groups are illustrated in the table below, with the main division being that Group 1 specialties recruit after IM3, and Group 2 specialties recruit a year earlier, after IM2.

Group 1 specialties will result in the trainee being dual trained in that specialty and General Internal Medicine. As such, the Consultants trained in these specialties will have responsibilities seeing patient populations within the specialty-specific population, but also be responsible for more general medical on call work. The extra year – IM3 – that Group 1 specialties have will see their trainees gain experience of being the Medical Registrar. The idea is that this will better prepare them for a career in a medical specialty that will also see them dual train in acute medicine.

The specialties that can recruit from IM2 are known as Group 2 specialties. Group 2 specialties will see their on call commitments mostly remaining consistent with current practise, although the exact curriculum is still being defined for some of the specialties.

Group 1 Specialties (Recruiting after IM3)	Group 2 Specialties (Recruiting after IM2)
Acute Internal Medicine	Allergy
Cardiology	Audio-Vestibular Medicine
Clinical Pharmacology & Therapeutics	Aviation & Space Medicine
Endocrinology and Diabetes Mellitus	Clinical Genetics
Geriatric Medicine	Clinical Neurophysiology
Gastroenterology	Clinical Oncology
Genitourinary Medicine	Dermatology
Infectious Diseases	Haematology
Neurology	Immunology
Palliative Medicine	Medical Ophthalmology
Renal Medicine	Nuclear Medicine
Respiratory Medicine	Occupational Medicine
Rheumatology	Paediatric Cardiology
Tropical Medicine	Pharmaceutical Medicine
	Rehabilitation Medicine
	Sport & Exercise Medicine

*Note: the decision regarding which group Medical Oncology belongs to has not yet been made

As you will no doubt identify, this is a momentous change in the way that postgraduate doctors are trained in the UK. The exact details will still take several years to confirm, but it is clear that the changes implemented by Shape of Training are attempting to help solve a critical problem posed by the changing population demographics of the UK. For further information, including the in-depth Internal Medicine Stage 1 curriculum, please visit the Joint Royal College of Physicians Training Board website.

The Main Changes in IM compared to CMT

Doctors entering the 2019 intake will be the first to commence IM training. This programme differs from CMT in a number of ways, and we will discuss these now: having an understanding of this may prove valuable at the interviews by showing you are up-to-date with recent events.

Internal Medicine Stage 1 will see several mandatory placements throughout the programme designed to address core goals of the Shape of Training reforms. These 'rules' are new compared to CMT, and include:

- a minimum of 4 months spent in Geriatric Medicine,
- a spell spent in Intensive Care (minimum duration spent in ICU being 10 weeks, but the aim is for all trainees to spend 3 months in ICU)
- specific Outpatient training (aiming for weekly or twice-weekly clinics at least throughout IM2).

As we mentioned above, however, the two training programmes remain mostly similar in their delivery of experience of the acute medical on call rota, completion of portfolio requirements, and progression in the MRCP(UK) qualification.

THE PERSON SPECIFICATION

The Internal Medicine person specification (see the Specialty Training Health Education England website at https://specialtytraining.hee.nhs.uk/) is a document released yearly that dictates the essential criteria and qualities that you must have achieved in order to be eligible to apply for Internal Medicine.

Being familiar with the person specification prior to completing your application is crucial. This will not only remind yourself of your core strengths and weaknesses (useful when completing white-box questions and preparing for potential interview topics), but it may also give you a chance to complete any missing aspects of your application. Importantly, it allows you to gain an understanding of **exactly** what the interviewers are looking for.

We will reproduce the person specification below. This should be used as a guide for what to include in the various sections of the application (particularly relevant when looking through the chapter of this book that covers the application form). These criteria are assessed using a combination of your application form, your portfolio of achievements, your performance during the interview itself, and your references.

The person specification is divided into two sections. The first deals with essential 'Entry Criteria': criteria that all applicants must possess in order to be eligible to apply. The second covers the 'Selection Criteria': criteria that provides the opportunity to differentiate between, and therefore rank, candidates. Obtaining a good ranking is of course critical, not only for ensuring you get accepted into the programme, but so that you get one of your top choices of rotations.

Part I: Entry Criteria

Category	Essential Criteria
Qualifications	Applicants must have MBBS or equivalent medical qualification

Eligibility	Applicants must:
	- be eligible for full registration with, and hold a current license to practice from the GMC at intended start date
	- have evidence of achievement of foundation competences, in the three and a half years preceding the advertised post start date for the round of application, via one of the following methods:
	  1. current employment in a UKFRO-affiliated Foundation Programme
	  2. 12 months experience after full GMC registration or equivalent, and evidence of achievement of Foundation competences at time of application
	- be eligible to work in the UK
	- have an Advanced Life Support Certificate from the Resuscitation Council UK or equivalent by intended start date

Fitness to Practice	Applicant is up to date and fit to practice safely and is aware of own training needs
Language skills	Applicants must have demonstrable skills in written and spoken English, adequate to enable effective communication about medical topics with patients and colleagues, as assessed by the General Medical Council
Health	Applicants must meet professional health requirements (in line with GMC standards / Good Medical Practice)
Career Progression	Applicants must: - be able to provide complete details of their employment history - have evidence that their career progression is consistent with their personal circumstances - have notified the training programme director of the specialty training programme they are currently training in if applying to continue training in the same specialty in another region - applicants must not have previously relinquished or been released/removed from a training programme in this specialty, except if they have received an ARCP outcome 1 or under exceptional circumstances - not previously resigned, been removed from, or relinquished a post of programme with resultant failure to gain the award of a FPCC, except under extraordinary circumstances and on the production of evidence of satisfactory outcome from appropriate remediation
Application Completion	All sections of application form completed fully according to written guidelines

Part II: Selection Criteria

Category	Essential Criteria	Desirable Criteria
Qualifications	MBBS or equivalent medical degree	MRCP(UK) Part I Additional related qualifications (intercalated degree, BA, BSc,)
Clinical Skills: Clinical Knowledge and Expertise	Ability to apply sound clinical knowledge and judgment to problems Ability to prioritise clinical need Ability to maximise safety and minimise risk Recognition of, and ability to undertake the initial management of, an acutely ill patient	
Research Skills, Audit and Teaching	Demonstrates understanding of research, including awareness of ethical issues Demonstrates understanding of the basic principles of audit, clinical risk management, evidence-based practice, patient safety, and clinical quality improvement initiatives Demonstrates knowledge of evidence-informed practice	Evidence of relevant academic and research achievements e.g. degrees, prizes, awards, distinctions, publications, presentations, other achievements Evidence of involvement in an audit project, quality improvement project, formal research project or other activity which focuses on patient safety and clinical improvement and demonstrates an interest in, and commitment to, the specialty beyond the mandatory curriculum Evidence of interest in, and experience of, teaching Evidence of feedback for teaching
Probity – Professional Integrity	Demonstrates probity (displays honesty, integrity, aware of ethical dilemmas, respects confidentiality) Capacity to take responsibility for own actions	
Commitment to Specialty – Learning and Personal Development	Shows initiative/drive/enthusiasm (self-starter, motivated, shows curiosity, initiative) Demonstrable interest in, and understanding of, the specialty Commitment to personal and professional development Evidence of attendance at organised teaching and training programme(s) Evidence of self-reflective practice	Extracurricular activities/achievements relevant to the specialty

Personal Skills	**Communication skills:** - demonstrates clarity in written/spoken communication, and capacity to adapt language to the situation as appropriate - able to build rapport, listen, persuade and negotiate **Problem solving & decision making:** - capacity to use logical/lateral thinking to solve problems/make decisions, indicating an analytical/scientific approach **Empathy and sensitivity:** - capacity to take in others' perspectives and treat others with understanding; sees patients as people - demonstrates respect for all Managing others & team involvement: - able to work in multi-professional teams and supervise junior medical staff - ability to show leadership, make decisions, organise and motivate other team members; for the benefit of patients through, for example, audit and quality improvement projects - capacity to work effectively with others **Organisation and planning:** - capacity to manage/prioritise time and information effectively - capacity to prioritise own workload and organise ward rounds - evidence of thoroughness (well-prepared, shows self-discipline/commitment, punctual and meets deadlines Vigilance and situational awareness: - capacity to monitor developing situations and anticipate issues	**Management & leadership skills:** - evidence of involvement in management commensurate with experience - demonstrates an understanding of NHS management and resources - evidence of effective multi-disciplinary team working and leadership, supported my multi-source feedback or other workplace-based assessments - evidence of effective leadership in and outside of medicine **IT skills:** - demonstrates information technology skills **Other:** - evidence of achievements outside medicine - evidence of altruistic behaviour e.g. voluntary work - evidence of organizational skills – not necessarily in medicine e.g. grant or bursary applications, organization of a university club, sports section etc **Coping with pressure & managing uncertainty:** - capacity to operate under pressure - demonstrates initiative and resilience to cope with challenging circumstances - is able to deliver good clinical care in the face of uncertainty **Values:** - understands, respects and demonstrates the values of the NHS (e.g. everyone counts, improving lives, commitment to quality of care, respect and dignity, working together for patients, compassion)

These are the criteria that your application (again, comprising your application form, portfolio, interview performance and references) will be judged upon. It is our goal to ensure that the rest of this book guides your application to enable it to showcase these criteria in an obvious and beneficial way. If you are able to do this then you will score very highly in both the application and the interview.

THE APPLICATION & SCORING

The application for IM involves the completion of an online application form (which involves ranking your own application against set criteria to give you an application score), the preparation of a portfolio to prove this ranking, and a subsequent interview.

We will first discuss the scoring system as applies to the online application and the interview itself to allow you gain an understanding of how places are offered.

We will then discuss the online application, including the evidence ranking system, and provide tips on how to maximise your ranking points. We then turn to a discussion of your portfolio, and how best to structure it to show off the evidence that you list in your application.

Finally, and for the remainder of the book, we will discuss the interview itself, covering the structure and advice for commonly occurring topics. By applying these principles to your application, you should feel much better prepared for the application, and this in turn should be reflected in your scores.

Application Scoring

You receive an application score based on your online application (discussed in detail in the next chapter). This score is entirely based on your self-ranking – but is checked by during the interview so you must be entirely honest or face potential GMC action. This is out of a value of 66, which is then multiplied by 0.25 to give a maximum score for the application of 16.5.

Your application score is added together with your interview score (covered in the next section) to give you an overall score, which is the score that determines if your application has been successful, and what your individual ranking is.

Interview Scoring

There are three interview stations at which you receive a score: Station 1 covering the portfolio, Station 2 covering a clinical scenario and communication skills, and Station 3 covering ethics and professionalism. At each station you receive scores in two categories (details will be covered in the chapter related to each interview station), and are scored by two interviewers, making 12 total scores available.

These values range from 1 – 5, and are outlined below:

Ranking	Descriptor
1	Candidate not appointable
2	Candidate performed below level of F2
3	Candidate performed at level of current F2
4	Candidate performed at level of completion of F2
5	Candidate performed at level of current IM Trainee

You must not score any '1's, and must not score more than two '2's in order to be deemed appointable. In addition, your total score must be greater than 36. As mentioned, each individual score is out of 5, with 12 individual scores given, and therefore there are a maximum of 60 points available. The final scores for each station are then multiplied by a specified factor (each station has a different multiplier), which gives a maximum available interview score of 80.

Your application score is then added to your interview score to give a final total score. This is the value that determines whether you have been successful in your application and what your ranking is.

As you can see, this is all somewhat confusing. We include a case example below to illustrate how this works.

Case Example:

John ranks himself as having achieved 40 points in the application. This is multiplied by 0.25 and gives him an application score of **10**.

John attends interview and achieves a total score of 44, and via the different multipliers his final interview score is **58**.

His total application score is 10 + 58 = **68**.

In his specific year of application, there were 100 places available in his top choice of deanery. The 100th best score of all applicants was 70, and therefore John was unfortunately not successful for this deanery. However, his second choice deanery had 120 places available, and the 120th best score of all applicants was 65. Therefore, John achieved a place within that deanery, and will be ranked based on his score within the 120 applicants when it comes to choosing his specific rotations.

Some candidates do not unfortunately achieve the minimum score they need in any of their ranked deaneries, or have a particularly bad time at interview which results in them being deemed 'not appointable' during the initial application. However, these applicants have another chance at achieving an IM place as they can then enter 'Round 2' of applications, as detailed below.

Round 2 Applications

Internal Medicine Stage 1 applications have two 'Rounds'. That means if you are unsuccessful in your application during the first Round you can still apply for the unfilled posts in Round 2. The Round 2 process usually starts in the middle of February, the year following the initial application, with advertisement of the unfilled posts.

A couple of weeks after this advertisement, the applications open. The application follows a nearly identical process to the Round 1 applications, with a similar online application being made, and high enough scoring candidates being invited to interview. The interviews themselves follow the same process as during the Round 1 applications, and are usually held during mid to late April.

Following the interview, successful candidates are notified and they will enter Internal Medicine Stage 1 with the rest of the cohort from Round 1 in August of that year.

THE ONLINE APPLICATION

We turn now to a discussion of the online application process. We cover the different sections of the application, and go into depth discussing the ways your application is ranked. Finally, we provide some suggestions on ways to maximise your application score. It is helpful in this chapter to refer back to the Person Specification to ensure your answers tick all the right boxes.

Internal Medicine Stage 1 – An Overview

The online application is completed through the NHS Oriel jobs advertising system (www.oriel.nhs.uk).

The Internal Medicine recruitment website provides much useful information regarding the application and interview process, as well as previous years' competition ratios.

We will cover below the eleven individual sections of the application, providing advice for the completion of each, before turning to the essential section of how to rank your portfolio.

1. *Personal*

This section serves as the introduction to your application, and is where you enter personal information about you such as contact information.

2. *Eligibility*

This section acts as a filter to ensure applicants only proceed if they meet the eligibility criteria: applicants must be eligible for a full license to practice from the General Medical Council. They must be eligible for residence and work in the United Kingdom, and must have sufficient English language skills. Full eligibility criteria can be read on the Health Education England website (https://specialtytraining.hee.nhs.uk/Recruitment/Person-specifications).

3. *Fitness*

This section asks about any prior criminal convictions that you may have, or any Fitness to Practice hearings that have been raised against you. Please see the General Medical Council's website for further guidance if you are unsure how to complete this section.

4. *References*

The IM application requires contact information for three referees (including your most recent consultant/educational supervisor) who have agreed to provide a clinical reference for you.

As with all job applications, the quality of reference is important – and your application cannot proceed without them. You should therefore contact your chosen referees with plenty of time to spare to ensure they are willing and able to provide your reference. It is worth noting that you will not see these references during the application, and so it is important to identify potential referees who you believe will provide a fair assessment of you as a clinician.

5. *Competences*

A medical degree is a required competency to enter IM: therefore, uploading evidence of this represents part of this section. You must also upload your certificate of Foundation competence – this is a certificate issued to you by your Foundation school following successful completion of the programme.

6. *Employment*

This section enables you to list your previous employment history for the past 3 years – if you plan to enter IM straight from the Foundation Programme then this will include details of your rotations along with their dates.

If you have taken a gap of longer than 28 days, then you will be required to enter information about your activities during these gaps in this section. A slight quirk is that if you entered the Foundation Programme straight from University, and are planning on entering IM straight from the Foundation Programme, then you will need to list a year-long 'employment gap', which represents your final undergraduate year of study.

7. *Evidence*

This section of the application is often viewed as the most challenging. This is where you self-rank your application against a set of pre-determined criteria that all applicants are ranked against. These criteria are: qualifications, prizes/awards, presentations, publications, quality improvement, teaching and leadership. We will discuss this critical stage in more detail in a subsequent section.

8. *Supporting*

This section allows you to add further supporting information to your application. The five sections include:

➤ **Academic Clinical Fellowship Applications** – if you have also applied for an ACF in this round of applications then you need to state this is the case here (so you can be clinically benchmarked). ACF applicants can select a box that results in their removal from the IM recruitment pool should they be unsuccessful in their application.

➤ **MRCP(UK) Examinations** – a desirable, though not essential, person specifications of IM applicants is to have passed some of the MRCP(UK) exams already. This section lets you detail these achievements.

➤ **Commitment to Specialty** – this is a white box question that lets you show what makes you committed to applying to IM. Your application score is not affected by this question, but the contents can and do come up at interview. You should use this opportunity to discuss your career aspirations, volunteering work you have done, conferences you have attended and quality improvement projects that you have participated in, all of which demonstrates your commitment to a career in medicine. We discuss this in detail in a later section.

➤ **Additional Achievements Outside of Medicine** – this is a further white box question that lets you briefly describe several achievements outside of medicine. You will link to these again in your portfolio, and choosing achievements that are particularly impressive and with good photographic evidence (e.g. of certificates or you in specific locations) provides good visual evidence for the examiners. Again, we cover these white box questions in a subsequent section.

➤ **Training Courses Attended** – you may list up to four training courses that you have attended which are of relevance to the IM application. Examples may include any modules of health-related Masters degrees that you have completed, or other clinical training courses such as Advanced Trauma Life Support (ATLS).

9. *Preferences*

This is a reminder that after the interview you will need to enter preferences for your choices of IM region.

10. *Equality*

This is a section designed for you to optionally enter information about your background.

11. *Declaration*

This final section confirms that you understand how your personal data will be used. You must also confirm again that all of the data and rankings that you have provided are true.

Section 7 – Evidence

This is the most important part of your application – it is where you rank yourself against set criteria, and is what contributes to your overall application score. We will cover what the examiners are looking for with regards to each section, and will provide advice on how to maximise the points you can achieve during your ranking. The scoring tables below are taken from the JRCPTB recruitment website but you are strongly advised to check their website for any updates.

Domain	Score	Description
Qualifications - Undergraduate	8	1st Class Honours degree or equivalent, achieved either as intercalated degree or prior to medical degree
	4	2.1 Class Honours degree or equivalent, achieved either as intercalated degree or prior to medical degree
	0	None
Qualifications - Postgraduate	10	PhD
	8	MD (2 year, research based)
	6	MPhil
	5	Single year postgraduate degree (MA, MRes etc)
	4	MD (dissertation only)
	3	Postgraduate diploma (between 1 and 10 months in duration)
	0	None
Prizes/Awards	8	National prize
	6	Honours/Distinction in medical degree
	4	>1 prize
	3	1 prize
	2	Scholarship/Bursary awarded in medical school
	0	None
Presentations	6	Oral presentation at national or international meeting
	6	>1 poster presentation at national or international meeting
	4	1 poster at national or international meeting
	4	Oral presentation at regional meeting
	3	1 or more posters at regional meeting
	2	Oral or poster presentation(s) at local meeting
	0	None
Publications (can include *in press*)	8	First author of 2 or more PubMed-cited original research publications
	7	Co-author of 2 or more PubMed-cited original research publications
	6	First author of 1 PubMed-cited paper original research publication
	5	Co-author of 1 PubMed-cited paper original research publication
	4	Author of >1 PubMed-cited 'other' articles, including case reports, letters and reviews
	3	Author of 1 PubMed-cited 'other' article, including case reports, letters and reviews
	2	Author of 1 or more abstracts or non-peer reviewed papers
	0	None
Teaching - Provision	7	Designed a local teaching programme over several sessions, lasting >3 months, and have formal feedback
	6	Organised a local teaching programme over more than one session, for >3 months, and have formal feedback
	4	Provided regular teaching to medical students over a period >3 months
	2	Occasional teaching, with formal feedback
	0	None

Teaching – Training In	3	Higher qualification in teaching (PG Cert etc)
	2	Official training in teaching lasting >2 days
	1	Brief training, <2 days or online modules
	0	None
Quality Improvement	10	Designed, led and implemented change as a result of QI project, and have presented the results
	8	Designed, led and implemented change as a result of QI project, but have not presented the results
	6	Actively participated in QI project and presented results at a meeting
	4	Actively participated in QI project but have not presented the results
	2	Participated only in certain stages of QI project
	0	None
Leadership	6	Held a national leadership/managerial role for >6 months as medical student or doctor
	4	Held a regional leadership/managerial role for >6 months as medical student or doctor
	2	Held a local leadership/managerial role for >6 months as medical student or doctor
	0	None

After ranking yourself based on the above criteria, you then need to provide several statements (in the form of a 'white box' style questions (covered in the next section)) that explain why, and provide evidence for, your specific choice of ranking.

How to Maximise Your Score

There are several tips that we will share which may allow you to increase your overall application score in a relatively short period of time.

Teaching Experience:

One of the areas of the application that applicants often struggle to fill out is the teaching experience section if they feel they don't have a great deal of teaching experience. There are a couple of tips for this. One is that you should look to see if there are any upcoming medical student OSCEs that you can examine at: you will be provided with a certificate and this is important teaching experience that can be included in your application.

If there are no OSCEs available to examine at then you can always provide some OSCE teaching for local medical students (who are always keen for teaching). Just remember to bring blank feedback forms for the students to complete after your session. If you are reading this 3 months prior to completing the application then you should aim for the higher marks within this section. It is easy to design a local teaching programme for medical students. For example, it could focus on teaching them the relevant system examinations that they will require for their OSCEs (including respiratory, cardiology, neurology, abdominal etc). The students could have a session every week or two, and you could design an exam at the end where you provide feedback for them and then give them a certificate of completion of the course. Sending an email to your local medical school would be a good way to get this registered. Even if you don't want to design a teaching course, you just need to have evidence of regular feedback forms from medical students (they will be included in your portfolio) for >3 months in order to score 4 marks in this section.

Teaching – Training In:

In terms of the training in teaching section, there is a free online course that can be completed in a couple of hours that provides training in teaching. It's freely available online (www.psychiatrycpd.co.uk/learningmodules/teachingclinicalskills.aspx) and will most certainly be the easiest points you'll be able to score. This can be a very useful way to increase the number of points you score in the application if you do not have previous experience of training in teaching.

Quality Improvement:

There are 4 marks for *'Actively participated in QI project but have not presented the results'* but 6 marks available for *'Actively participated in QI project and presented results at a meeting'*. If you have completed a QI project but not yet presented it then it would be wise to try to look for ways that you can present the results (this will be most valid if you are reading the book in advance of the application date, of course). Note that there is not a specific caliber of meeting required: this does not have to be a large international meeting. Therefore, look for regional or local subspecialty or QI meetings, or departmental meetings where you may be able to present the results of your QI project at. If you can facilitate this, these are two easy points to get.

Presentations:

If you have no evidence of presentations on your portfolio then look for some upcoming local meetings that you can present the findings of your Foundation Programme QI project. This is another relatively straightforward 2 marks to achieve if you have the time before the application deadline.

Section 8 – Supporting Information: 'White Box Questions'

Throughout Section 8 there are several 'white box' questions that allow you to compose your own answer to the question posed. These are important: they are the only chance to really demonstrate your own achievements in your own words (since the prior sections rely on you ranking your achievements against pre-set criteria). In particular, the 'Commitment to Specialty' answer is quite important. It is an answer that the interviewers may refer to before looking through your portfolio, as it is an easy way for them to obtain an overview of your achievements.

We now list each of the different questions that have been present in Section 8, and provide advice for how to answer them most effectively.

Achievements Outside Medicine

Describe any achievements outside of the field of medicine which you would like to include in support of your application. It is not mandatory to enter any information here but is recommended to refer to the person specification when considering information to include (maximum 150 words):

This is a question that gives you a good opportunity to highlight how you fill a lot of the Selection Criteria within the Person Specification. Discuss sporting achievements, clubs that you have been involved in (and potentially taken leadership and management roles in such as secretary, treasurer or president), voluntary work you have done (doesn't have to be medicine related), prizes you may have won in non-medicine related activities and other non-medical qualifications you have gained (for example, musical instruments, scuba diving etc). All of these examples will show that you satisfy different aspects of the Person Specification (that you are a 'self-starter', have 'drive', have previously engaged in 'altruistic behaviour', and have good evidence of 'organisational skills').

Additional Undergraduate Degrees and Qualifications

Please include details of the qualification awarded, institution/awarding body and dates (100 words):

This is a fairly self-explanatory question: list the graduation date, University and degree (or other qualification) name for your degrees that contribute to your self-ranking score in Section 7 (see previous section of this book).

Postgraduate Degrees and Qualifications

Please include details of the qualification awarded, institution/awarding body and dates (_100 words_):

As with the previous question, use this space to list any postgraduate degrees and qualifications that you may have (including PhDs, MDs and MPhils that you have gained since graduating from medical school.

Additional Training Course Information

If you would like to add information about any additional training courses which you have attended which you think are particularly relevant and not mentioned above, please use the space provided. It is not mandatory to do this and recommended only to include courses which are most relevant (100 words):

Use this section to include courses that may not be official qualifications as such but which are relevant to your future career and which show further evidence of your commitment to a career in a medical specialty. This may include specialist clinical courses (such as Advanced Trauma and Life Support), specific modules of masters degrees that you have completed or other postgraduate diplomas.

Additional Achievements

Please specify any honours degrees, prizes, awards and other distinctions you have gained (100 words):

This question is looking for further information about the ranking you gave yourself in the Prizes/Awards topic of Section 7 (see previous section of this book). List the name of the prize, the body awarding it, the date it was awarded, and, if you have space, briefly the reasons that you were awarded the prize.

Presentations/Posters

Please provide details of your most relevant presentations and/or posters. Please give a statement about your personal contribution to the work (350 words):

As the question states, this is not the opportunity to list every presentation that you have ever given to fellow medical students or during your undergraduate career. We would recommend listing the achievements in the following order:

1. Oral presentation(s) at international conferences
2. Oral presentation(s) at national and regional conferences
3. Poster presentation(s) at international conferences
4. Poster presentation(s) at national and regional conferences
5. Oral presentation(s) at local meetings (grand round presentations, presentations to your department on QI projects
6. Poster presentation(s) at local meetings (University medical school conferences, local quality improvement meetings, journal clubs)

Fill up the space in this question by first discussing examples of Number 1, then 2, the 3 etc with sufficient detail to let the question marker understand what the presentation was about until you run out of space. Don't deliberately go too light on the detail so that you can fill in your local presentations. Look at what mark you scored yourself in Section 7 (for example, if you scored 6 for >1 poster presentation at national or international meeting then discuss those posters first and fully before moving onto less impressive presentations (especially given that they don't influence your application score).

Do not forget the second-half of the question: you are expected to discuss your personal contribution to the work. This can include (but isn't limited to) project inception, project design, obtaining ethical approval, experimental design, performing experiments, data collection, data analysis and writing up the project into the form of posters/talks/papers.

Publications

Please provide details of your most relevant publications. Please give full citation details (as in Pubmed (http://www.ncbi.nlm.nih.gov/pubmed)) of any published work and then give a statement about your personal contribution to the work. If adding details of an abstract, please add '(abstract)' as a note (300 words):

This question provides the evidence for the Publications component of Section 7. The highest score is 8, and is awarded for being first author of 2 or more PubMed-cited original research publications. The first thing to say is that the majority of candidates will not have any publications, and if they do, they will not fulfill this top score category: therefore don't worry if you don't have any publication.

If you do, then I would list them from the highest impact publication down to the lowest impact: you want to always lead with your most impressive achievement.

As above, do not forget the second-half of the question: you are expected to discuss your personal contribution to the work. This can include (but isn't limited to) project inception, project design, obtaining ethical approval, experimental design, performing experiments, data collection, data analysis and writing up the project into the form of posters/talks/papers.

Cite papers in the following format (as they appear on PubMed):

> Citation: *de la Roche M, et al. Hedgehog signalling controls T cell killing at the immunological synapse. Science. 2013 Dec 6;342(6163):1247-50*

Cite each paper after the discussion on that paper before turning to a discussion on the next chapter. If you have space left in the word count then you can also include the link to the PubMed listing (for the above example, this would be: https://www.ncbi.nlm.nih.gov/pubmed/24311692).

Teaching Experience

Please provide details of your teaching experience. Please give full details about the type of teaching, your personal contribution, details of any feedback obtained and how you have reflected on this (250 words):

In this question you should discuss the different types of teaching experience that you have gained throughout your time in medical school and on the Foundation Programme. This may include having a formal role teaching more junior medical students, being an academic advisor to being involved in OSCE teaching courses where you may have given multiple teaching sessions to medical students about how to (for example) examine patients.

Discuss how you collected feedback from your students. Was it verbal or written, and if written did you have a form that you gave to students after the session? Written feedback is always best, so try to discuss that if that is what you did. A part of the question that candidates sometimes for get to discuss is the *'and how you have reflected on this'* section. Therefore, give examples of how you looked through the feedback you were given, and how you then adapted future teaching sessions to the requests or suggestions of the students (this can be as simple as: *the students felt the teaching sessions were too short and a little rushed and so I therefore changed to having them at the end of the day which meant I was less pressured in my job and could spend more time with the students. The subsequent feedback that I received suggests that this was a popular change*).

Training in Teaching

Please provide details of your training in teaching. Include details about the course provider, any qualification gained, start and end dates, the length of training and the how the course was conducted (100 words):

This is your opportunity to discuss what training in teaching you have had. If you taught medical students OSCE techniques did you have any introductions by the medical school? If you were an Academic Advisor did you have teaching sessions from the University about what your role involved? If you've used an online module then also discuss that here (see our advice on 'How to Maximise Your Score').

Quality Improvement

Please provide details of your experience of quality improvement projects, giving titles and dates. What specifically was your contribution, what did the audit show, was the audit presented or published and was the audit cycle closed (250 words):

All applicants should have at least one Quality Improvement project (if not two) that they have been involved in given the requirements of the Foundation Programme. This is your opportunity to discuss them in detail. As mentioned, you should start by giving the title of the project(s) and dates it was performed over. Then discuss the main findings of the project and the difference that you were (or were not) able to make. Mention whether the findings were presented (whether this is simply at departmental clinical governance meetings in the hospital where you performed the project, or at a national meeting). Finally, discuss your role in the project, from project design, to data collection and analysis, to implementing change and presenting the findings.

It can be helpful to be familiar with some of the key terminologies of QI projects in this section: if you are able to discuss that you were able to meet your SMART aim using several different approaches, each of which followed PDSA model, then it will be clear to the examiners that you are up to date with QI methodology and committed to making positive changes to clinical practice. We will discuss QI projects in more detail in the chapter covering the Portfolio section of the interview, but a brief recap will remind you of some of the key phrases to include in your answer.

The SMART (Specific, Measurable, Achievable, Relevant and Time-Bound) acronym provides a structure to forming a modern QI methodology aim. The aim (and its individual components) is designed to allow the investigators to develop a project that is likely to be completed and to come out with results within a known timeframe. An example would be: _We aim to reduce the incidence of hospital acquired venous thromboembolism by 90% by August 2019._

The PDSA (planning, doing, studying, acting and returning to planning) cyclical model is the approach that should underpin each of the changes implemented in the QI project. It is inherently reflective in nature: so in the above example, if we were assessing the incidence of venous thromboembolism each month, then we would perform a PDSA cycle at the end of each month to determine the areas that need to be improved on in the subsequent month.

Commitment to Specialty

Describe how you believe you meet the person specification for the programme for which you are applying. Include the particular skills and attributes that make you suitable for a career in this specialty.

Use the space to provide fresh supporting information rather than repeating the information you have already provided in previous sections. Your answer in this section will not contribute to your short-list score, but commitment to specialty is a significant part of the interview so, should you be invited, your answer may be discussed at that stage (400 words):

This is an important question as it often provides the basis for a lot of what you will be asked in the portfolio station interview. You should use this section to highlight different things you have done that show you have been working towards a career in any medical specialty, and that highlight how you meet many of the 'Selection Criteria' of the person specification.

You will not be penalised if you don't know which specialty you want to apply for. This question is designed for you to show how you would make a good IM trainee and not a good trainee in (e.g.) cardiology. The latter, of course, is the purpose of the ST3 applications.

If you do know what specialty you want to apply for then feel free to discuss it and the things you have done that have shown that that specialty is the career path you want to take. This may include conferences that you have attended and extra clinical experience that you have organised (such as taster days/weeks).

Sitting (and ideally passing) MRCP(UK) exams also indicates that you have a serious commitment to a medical career. Therefore, you can briefly (briefly, because you have space in the above questions to discuss them) mention any professional exams that you have passed here. You should also include professional courses in this answer, which show further evidence of commitment to specialty. This will also highlight your *'commitment to personal and professional development'* (another component of the person specification).

You may have received glowing compliments from senior doctors or other team members during your time on the Foundation Programme (especially useful if documented in your portfolio – consider looking through your team based assessments or multi-source feedback for quotes you can use). Don't be afraid to highlight them here, especially if they mention that they think you will make a good IM trainee (for example). You may also have received 'thank you' cards or notes from patients, the contents of which may also indicate that you are well suited to a career in a medical specialty. These cards (so long as not patient-identifiable) should then be included in your portfolio (see the next chapter).

One specific topic in the person specification worth highlighting is *'shows initiative/drive/enthusiasm (self-starter, motivated, shows curiosity, initiative)'*. Try and have this in mind when completing this answer: for example, showing that you've arranged taster days or weeks shows your drive and enthusiasm, taking leadership positions (e.g. the mess committee, or British Medical Association representatives) shows initiative and drive, and feedback from senior doctors may mention your initiative and drive.

Other aspects mentioned in the person specification that are worth including here include evidence of *'attendance at organised teaching'* (you could include a brief sentence discussing your engagement with teaching during your Foundation Programme, including the percentage of sessions that you attended (so long as it is impressive e.g. above 90%)), *'evidence of altruistic activity'* (discuss any voluntary work that you have done) and *'demonstrates information technology skills'* (you could have a brief sentence to discuss your prowess in relevant computer software packages or if you have any experience of coding which may help you when performing and analysing quality improvement projects).

PREPARING THE PORTFOLIO

In this chapter we will focus on how to prepare and structure your portfolio. Something many people, myself included, are surprised to first learn is that this is a physical portfolio – usually presented in large ring binder – that you bring with you to the interview. You fill this with relevant certificates and proof of your achievements and bring it with you. Therefore, planning this well in advance is highly recommended, as it takes a surprisingly long time to locate and print the required evidence to prove your claims (see the previous chapter).

The Portfolio

Before going into your interview your portfolio will be taken from you. The examiners have a very short period of time to look through this before they call you into the portfolio station. Therefore, the key to success is making your examiners do the absolute minimum amount of work required to validate what you said in your application, and to make it easy for them to find everything they need to see how good an applicant you are.

We would recommend a large black folder with ring binders inside. You should include a label on the front of the folder with the required identification information (in previous years this has included your full name, Application ID and GMC number). We would recommend that you use coloured chapter dividers to allow the examiners to easily move between sections. You should also invest in a large number of poly-pockets to store your certificates. They make it easier for the examiners to turn the pages and prevent your certificates from becoming damaged.

We now present a recommended structure for your portfolio. There is no one correct way to structure it, but this method has been used by top ranked candidates and therefore has been shown to be successful.

Contents

On the inside front cover insert a contents page that makes reference to the chapter/page dividers. Take, for example, *2. Additional Achievements*. To make this easy to find, have an obviously labelled divider with a large number '2', which the examiners can then turn to and find your additional achievements.

Opposite the contents page you should have a copy of your *Curriculum Vitae*.

The individual sections should then be listed as follows:

1. Undergraduate Degrees & Qualifications
2. Additional Achievements
3. Presentations (First: Poster Presentations, Second: PowerPoint)
4. Publications
5. Teaching experience
6. Training in teaching
7. Quality improvement
8. Commitment to Specialty
9. Achievements outside Medicine
10. Training Courses Attended
11. Personal References and TAB Feedback

1. Undergraduate Degrees & Qualifications

In this section have the original degree certificates for your undergraduate medical degree. If you have them, include any additional degree certificates (BSc, BA, Masters, PhD etc). Also include your provisional GMC registration certificate.

2. Additional Achievements

In this section include any prizes won at undergraduate level, at conferences, or indeed any competitive scholarships that you won. If your name features within a list of other names then you should highlight your name (using a highlighting pen) to make it easy for the examiners to identify your achievement.

You can also include your degree transcript in this section if you scored particularly well/achieved a first class degree, or Honours/Distinction etc.

You may include in this section certificates from any successfully passed MRCP exams, though they are also suited to section 8.

3. Presentations (First: Poster Presentations, Second: PowerPoint)

Here you should include evidence of any poster presentations you have given at international, national and local conferences. I would include a printout the poster itself and on the reverse of the poster include the email or letter with confirmation of the poster having been accepted into the conference where it was presented (such that this is visible when turning the poly-pocket over).

You should then include a selection of your most impressive oral presentations by printing the PowerPoint files – I recommend printing these as '6 slide per page handouts' to ensure there isn't an excessive number of pages for the examiners to look through. Ensure the title of the project and the location and date of where you presented (e.g. Grand Round, My Hospital, 1st February 2018) in the first slide so the examiners understand the level of presentation. Again, feel free to highlight sections that are of particular importance or are impressive (e.g. the name of the conference if it was at an international conference).

4. Publications

Include the first page of any publications you have authored or co-authored. Highlight your name within the author list. On the reverse page of the poly pocket you could also include a printout of the abstract page from PubMed.

If you have mentioned papers that you have submitted but are not yet accepted then you should print out confirmation of the submission page from the journal's editorial team.

5. Teaching experience

This section is designed to show off the experience you have of teaching at both a graduate and undergraduate level. This can be a challenge to show off accurately, and therefore you should ensure you obtain feedback forms from students you have taught in formal training sessions. If you don't have any, then ask your local medical education department for a teaching feedback form template and contact your students asking them to fill in their information.

If you plan to give more teaching prior to preparing this portfolio then ensure you go to your sessions with feedback forms in hand so your students can fill them in immediately after the teaching session.

Useful tip – we mentioned this earlier, but it is worth repeating: being an OSCE examiner can be used as an example of teaching experience, and you will be provided with certificates for any OSCEs that you help examine at.

6. Training in teaching

This section is where you will show off any training in teaching you have had. This can be quite a challenging section to complete. Check back through your undergraduate clinical degree as some Universities include mandatory 'teacher training' courses, which are very valuable evidence for this section.

If you have attended any Multiple Choice Question writing sessions for medical student exams then you will have had training as part of that process, and therefore a certificate from this session is valid in this section.

If you act as an 'Academic Advisor' for undergraduate medical students during your time as a Foundation Doctor then you will receive training in how to fulfil this role – therefore include the certificates that document this as that also is useful teacher teaching experience.

Useful tip – we also discussed this earlier, but it is worth repeating. There are online courses that can be classed as courses for learning how to teach effectively. This can be a very useful means of increasing your total application score.

7. Quality improvement

Include certificates of evidence for completed QI projects/audits – either that were done during medical school or during the Foundation years. As completing one QI project/audit is mandatory for progression from F1 to F2 you should have at least one you can provide here!

8. Commitment to Specialty

You can include any successfully passed MRCP exam certificates in this section, as this demonstrates your commitment to a career in a medical specialty.

If you did any relevant volunteering work or clinically oriented projects during summers at University or during your elective then that is also useful and relevant to include here.

If you have attended any conferences – even if you didn't present there – then that is also a sign that you are committed to a career in a medical specialty. You should include your registration certificates in this section for these conferences.

9. Achievements outside Medicine

There are several ways of filling this section in, but remember that the examiners have a very limited amount of time with each portfolio and therefore visual impact and ease of reading are key. You could print 2 – 4 photos at half page size, which show you in a visually interesting area/show some form accomplishment with a small (one line) caption beneath explaining the achievement.

If you have certificates outside of the medical field (for example, in martial arts) then include them here. Similarly, include evidence of any particularly impressive sporting achievements here.

10. Training Courses Attended

This section overlaps with section 6 somewhat, but ensure you don't duplicate what you show here. Include online modules that are relevant

Useful tip – the BMJ website has interesting and short online e-learning modules that are relevant to many different medical careers, and the certificates provided upon completion can be included here.

11. Personal References and TAB Feedback

If you have received references from Directors' of Studies, or other supervisors, in the past for application to relevant scholarships/prizes/labs then you can include these here (providing you have agreement from the person providing the reference).

Similarly to the QI project discussed in Section 7, a Team Based Assessment is required for successful progression from F1 to F2. If you received nice feedback then you should feel free to include that in this section, ensuring it is appropriately anonymised.

Finally, if you have received any card from patients thanking you for your care then you can also include them here – with the essential caveat that you ensure no patient confidentiality is breached.

The Eligibility Folder

You actually need to bring two folders with you to the interview. However, you will be pleased to hear, the second folder – the Eligibility folder – is much easier to assemble than the evidence portfolio.

This is a folder that confirms your eligibility to apply for IM, and will be checked prior to your interview on the day itself. You must include a number of identification documents and degree certificates in this folder, as documented below. If you wish to include the same certificate in both this folder and your portfolio then you should make a copy, include the original in the eligibility folder, and place the copy in your evidence portfolio.

Eligibility evidence required:

1. Photographic Identification: use your passport here, making photocopies of the relevant pages as identified by the application website. You should expect the deanery to keep the copies.

2. Evidence Showing you can work in the UK: this shouldn't affect most UK applicants –as they will have a UK passport – but if you were not born in the UK then you need to provide evidence that you can work in the UK. This may be your passport, visa information or Home Office letters.

3. GMC Registration: you need to provide evidence of current registration with the GMC (if you are registered at the time of application). **Current** evidence means printing your name from the register (use the GMC website) with a timestamp that is within 7 days of the interview date.

GENERAL INTERVIEW ADVICE

Before we turn to a detailed discussion of the IM interview, we will first discuss some general interview advice covering preparing for the interview, how to act in the interview, and how to answer questions. As we mentioned, this is going to be the first interview in quite some time for many candidates at IM, and so it never hurts to go over some general tips for success.

How Do I Prepare for the Interview?

You have prepared yourself well for this interview simply by completing medical school and engaging with the Foundation Programme. You already have all of the information that you need. Following the advice presented in this book is useful for preparation – but the most useful preparation you can do is to have a practice interview.

Ask local consultants and registrars in your hospital if they would be willing to organise a brief practise interview for you. You would be surprised at how many of your senior colleagues will go out of their way to organise this one lunch or day after work for you. Practice interviews are best with someone you do not know very well - even easy questions may be harder to articulate out loud and on the spot to a stranger.

A practice interview lets you have a go at some of the portfolio questions that you have prepared in advance and see if they work for you under an interview circumstance. Your consultants will then be able to give you feedback on these answers, which will be invaluable when tweaking your answers to be the best they can be. In addition, being put under pressure with an unfamiliar clinical scenario will stand you in excellent stead when it comes to that section of the interview. During your practice interview, try to eliminate hesitant words like "Errrr...." and "Ummm..." as these will make you appear less confident. Ask for feedback on the speed, volume, and tone of your voice.

A second extremely useful way of preparing is to attend a locally run IM interview preparation day. If you don't know if your local deanery has these then ask some people in the above years and the teaching organisers if they know about any days like this. If you still can't find any, then you can also ask friends in neighbouring deaneries if they know preparation days being run where they are. These days are typically run in larger groups than any mock interviews you might organise, but they give another opportunity to practice your interview skills and get feedback on your answers.

Professionalism and Dress-Code

Remembering that the Consultants holding the interviews are looking for their future Registrars and Consultant colleagues, it is vital that you maintain a professional approach before, during and after the interview. You should make sure you arrive early at your destination. You should plan the route well in advance, and if you are unsure about the complexities of the journey then it is always wise to make a practice journey prior to the interview.

Make sure you are always polite and courteous to the interviewers. This is an opportunity for the interviewers to assess how you will fit in with their clinical team, and knowing that you are a polite and professional individual with good communication skills goes a long way to reassuring them of this.

Dress in smart attire – you can't go wrong with dress suits. Think about how formal most of the Consultants you have worked with in the past have been. It is important to give off the impression that you are ready to work with them at their level, and therefore dressing the part does make an impact when they are considering the overall suitability of a candidate.

Things to avoid:
➢ Excessively shiny or intricate jewellery
➢ Bold and controversial dress colours, e.g. orange ties
➢ Excessive amounts of makeup
➢ Flashy nails or eyelashes

Things to do:
➢ Carry an extra pair of contact lenses or glasses if appropriate
➢ Turn your phone off completely – you don't want any distractions
➢ Polish your shoes

Body Language

First impressions last; body language contributes to a significant part of this. However, don't make the mistake of obsessing over body language at the expense of the quality answers you give.

Posture
➢ When walking into the room, walk in with your head held high and back straight.
➢ When sitting down, look alert and sit up straight.
➢ Avoid crossing your arms – this can appear to be defensive.
➢ Don't slouch- instead, lean forward slightly to show that you're engaged with the interview.
➢ If there is a table, then ensure you sit around four to six inches away.
  ❖ Too close and you'll appear like you're invading the interviewers' space
  ❖ Too far and you'll appear too casual

Eyes
➢ Good eye contact is a sign of confidence and good communication skills.
➢ Look at the interviewer when they are speaking to you and when you are speaking.
➢ If there are multiple interviewers, look at the interviewer who is speaking to you or asked you the question. However, make sure you do look around at the other interviewers to acknowledge them.

Hands
➢ At the start, offer a handshake or accept if offered: make sure you don't have sweaty or cold hands.
➢ A firm handshake is generally preferable to a limp one.
➢ During the interview, keep your hands still unless you are using them to illustrate your point.
➢ Avoid excessive hand movements – your hands should go no higher than your neck.
➢ If you fidget when you're nervous, hold your hands firmly together in your lap to stop this from happening.

How to Communicate Answers

Our objective is not to state exactly how you should answer every interview question you come across. We will provide here some general advice that has proved useful to us – and our students – in interviews thus far, and which will provide a good basis for you when structuring your answers. A good way to ensure you consistently deliver effective answers is to adhere to the principles below:

Keep it Short:

In general, most your responses should be approximately one to two minutes long. They should convey the important information but be focussed on the question and avoid rambling. Remember, you are providing a direct response to the question, not writing an English essay! With practice, you should be able to identify the main issues being asked, plan a structured response, and communicate them succinctly. It's important to practice your answers to common questions, e.g. *'Why Apply for Internal Medicine Stage 1?'* so that you can start to get a feel for what is the correct response duration.

An example of this is a question I received at the start of one of my recent interviews. The question was : *"What jobs have you done as part of the Foundation Programme"*. At first I thought this was an opportunity to discuss those I liked, and the main lessons I learned in each job. However, I swiftly realized that this was a question designed to settle me into the interview, and the panel simply wanted to know exactly what they asked: a brief list of the jobs that I had done.

Give Examples:

Generic statements don't carry much weight without evidence to back them up. As a general rule, every statement that you make should be evidenced using examples. Consider the following statements:
Statement 1: *"I have good organisational skills."*
Statement 2: *"I have good organisational skills as evidenced by my ability to continue with my academic work throughout my clinical training. I published a paper last year, and was able to complete two quality improvement projects. I was also able to remain the treasurer of my local football team. The experiences have shown me the importance of good organisational skills in my future career."*

Think Before Answering:

Don't be afraid to take a pause before the start of your answer, particularly if the question is challenging or unexpected. The interviewers appreciate an applicant who takes time to think of an intelligent or thoughtful answer more than an applicant who blurts out the first thing that comes to mind, or one who doesn't answer at all because they become stressed that they can't answer immediately. You should, however, let your interviewers know that this is what you are doing. Say *"I'm going to think about this for a moment"*, or *"that's a good question, I need to think about that for a second before answering"*. Don't take too long: if you are finding the problems difficult, the **interviewers will guide and prompt you** to keep you moving forward. They can only do this if they realise you're stuck!

Answer the Question:

This cannot be stressed enough – there are few things more frustrating than students that ignore the interviewer's questions. Remember, you need to **answer the question**; **don't answer the topic**. If a question consists of two parts – remember to answer both.

Structuring your Answers

You can approach questions by using a simple framework:

A good when answering questions about personal attributes or skills can be to try and tick off each of these in your answer. This is a good way to ensure that you are not spending too long talking about one thing and so leaving yourself no time to talk about other things. There is little point in reeling off a list of unrelated facts when that would leave no time to show how your experiences apply.

It is better to demonstrate good knowledge and then move on to describe how insights from your prior experiences have also influenced you to give a more well-rounded answer. It's worth practising answering questions using this framework.

For example, consider: *'What do you think is the greatest challenge of being an IM doctor?'*

1. What knowledge can I apply?
IM doctors work challenging on call rotas. I know they have progressed to a position of increased responsibility compared to the Foundation Years. I know the structure of the training programme, which I might be able to work into the answer, and I know they have to progress through MRCP(UK) in order to successfully complete the IM programme.

2. What experiences can I use?
I remember seeing a lot of IM-level doctors looking tired on during F1. I remember one IM complaining that he was not getting to apply much of his medical knowledge, but instead felt like a secretary. I remember another IM doctor telling me that it was scary but an interesting challenge to be in a position where they have to make decisions – particularly when on call – about the management of patients.

3. What positive qualities can I display?
I can show a realistic understanding of the challenges of post-graduate medical training. I can show a diligent and conscientious attitude towards the challenge of hard work and long hours. I can show an ability to handle stress.

4. How can I give a balanced answer?
I should recognise that there are multiple factors that make IM a challenge in order to balance the answer.

You can go through a thought process like this in a few seconds and continue to think about it as you begin to answer the question. Thus, your answer may be along the lines of:

"There are clearly lots of different factors that are challenging for an IM doctor. For a start, the on call commitments will be a challenge to balance with the required progress through professional examinations. When I was an FY1, I remember an IM-level doctor telling me that the thing she found most challenging was the increase in responsibility and expectations between when she started her training programme. It was this that she and her peers found most stressful."

You can see how you have to be very picky about what you include in your answer to make sure you give a well-rounded answer in the tight time limit of the interview. For the same question, another response could focus on striking a work-life balance as being most challenging:

"During my F1 year, I saw IM doctors working long hours and busy shifts. In addition, they had to study for additional exams to ensure their career progression. This meant that the weekends were spent either on calls or attending courses. All this limited their social life. Thus, I think striking a good work-life balance could be challenging but possible with forward planning."

The STARR Framework

You may be asked questions where you need to give examples, e.g. *"Tell me about a time when you showed leadership?"*

It's very useful to **prepare examples in advance** for these types of questions, as it's very difficult to generate them on the spot. Try to **prepare at least three examples** that you can use to answer a variety of questions. Generally, more complex examples can be used to demonstrate multiple skills, e.g. communication, leadership, team-working, etc.

In the initial stages, it's helpful to use a framework to structure your answers, e.g. the STARR Framework shown below:

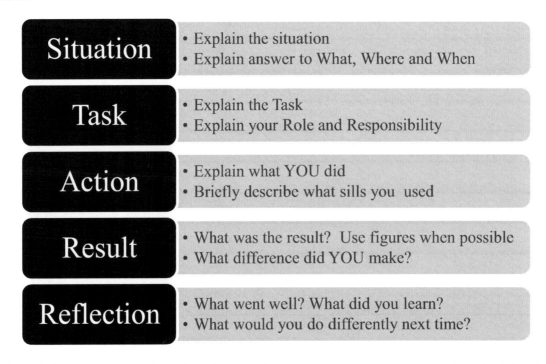

Situation	• Explain the situation • Explain answer to What, Where and When
Task	• Explain the Task • Explain your Role and Responsibility
Action	• Explain what YOU did • Briefly describe what sills you used
Result	• What was the result? Use figures when possible • What difference did YOU make?
Reflection	• What went well? What did you learn? • What would you do differently next time?

We will discuss examples of questions that benefit from using the STARR framework during later chapters, particularly in the chapter covering the Portfolio Station of the interview.

What Are the Interviewers Looking For?

Many applicants think that the most 'obvious' thing interviewers are looking for is excellent factual knowledge. This simply isn't true. As we discussed, the interviewers want to know if you are someone who can work well as their Registrar or colleague in the future. As such, they want to know that you possess a number of important personal traits. These include, but are not limited to:

Diligence

Medicine is a very demanding profession and – as you already know! – requires hard work throughout your career. Interviewers are looking not only for your ability to work hard (diligence) but also for an understanding that there will be times where you will have a responsibility to prioritise your medical work over other personal and social concerns (conscientiousness).

Professional Integrity

Medicine is a profession where lives could be at risk if something goes wrong. Being honest and having strong moral principles is critical for doctors. The public trusts the medical profession and this can only be maintained if there is complete honesty between both parties. Interviewers need to see that you are an honest person, can accept your mistakes and are learn from them.

Empathy

Empathy is the ability to recognise and relate to other peoples' emotional needs. It is important that you understand and respond appropriately to patients, relatives and colleagues in a variety of challenging situations. The easiest way to demonstrate this is by recalling situations from your previous experiences as a doctor (one of the many reasons why it's so important). However, it's important to not exaggerate how much an incident has affected you - experienced interviewers will quickly pick up on anything that doesn't sound sincere.

Resilience to Stress

There is no denying the fact that the Foundation Programme is stressful due to the extreme pressure you have been put under at varying times. The interviewers will themselves have been through these stages, and know that the levels of stress can increase as your responsibility increases, and therefore it's important that you have a way of dealing with it in a healthy manner. Interviewers are looking to see if you are able to make logical decisions when put under pressure. Pursuing interests outside of medicine, such as sport, music or drama is often a good way of de-stressing and gives you an opportunity to talk about your extra-curricular interests as well as team-working skills.

Self-Awareness

It's important to be able to recognise your own strengths and weaknesses. In addition, you need to be able to recognise and reflect on your mistakes so that you can learn from them for the future. A person with good self-awareness can work on their weakness to avoid mistakes from happening again. Questions like, "What are your strengths?" or "What is your biggest weakness?" are common and fantastic opportunities to let your maturity and personal insight shine through.

Teamwork and Leadership

Working as a doctor requires working in a multidisciplinary team (MDT) – a group of individuals with a wide variety of skills that work to help patients. The MDT is a cornerstone of how modern healthcare functions. Thus, you need to be able to show that you're a team player. One of the best ways of doing this is by giving examples from your extracurricular activities and from experiences on the wards over the last two years.

Interviewer Styles

Although interviewers have wildly different styles, it is helpful to remember that none of them are trying to catch you out. They are there to help you. You may come across an interviewer that is very polite and 'noddy' while others may have a 'poker face'. Do not be put off by their expressions or reactions. Sometimes what you thought was a negative facial response to your reply may just be a twitch. Contrastingly, a very helpful appearing interviewer may lull you into a false sense of security. Rarely, you may get an interviewer who likes playing 'Devil's advocate' and will challenge your every statement. In these cases, it's important not to take things personally and avoid getting worked up.

You don't know what type of interviewer you will get so it's important to practice mock interviews with as many people as possible so that you're prepared for a wider variety of interviewer styles.

Ending the Interview

At the end of the interview, the interviewers may ask you if you have any questions for them. Asking an intelligent question shows that you really care about what you are applying for and where you are applying to do it, and will always come across better than not asking anything. However, don't ask simple filler questions that could be solved by a quick internet search. Your questions should be insightful, and may be about a topic that only consultants familiar with the specific deanery can answer.

You should prepare at least three different questions prior to the interview, in case you are asked at the end of each of the three stations. Example questions include:

"Do your trainees have a set teaching programme, or is this decided based on what the group of trainees feels will be most useful to learn?"

"Do you find that consultants in the hospitals are often willing to provide support and training for the MRCP(UK) examinations?"

"I am interested in applying for infectious diseases, and wondered if you know if it is possible to use study days to arrange for taster weeks within this speciality? I ask because I know that infectious diseases within this deanery is very highly regarded."

"I am extremely interested in research, and want to gain more clinical trials research experience. Your deanery has a well-regarded trials centre, and I wondered if it were possible for trainees to arrange some outpatient experience within this to satisfy the clinic attendance requirements?"

These questions are just examples – the most genuine questions will be those that come from you and are directly related to your interests.

At the end of the interview, look the interviewers in the eye and thank them for their time. You are then free to leave, having completed the interview for Internal Medicine Stage 1.

Final Advice

1) **Don't be put off by what other candidates say** in the waiting room. Focus on yourself – you are all that matters. If you want to be in the zone, then I would recommend taking some headphones and your favourite music.

2) **Don't lose heart** if your interviews appear to have gone poorly. If anything, this can actually be a good sign as it shows that the interviewer pushed you to your limits.

3) **Don't give up.** When you're presented with complex scenarios, go back to the absolute basics and try to work things out using first principles. By doing this and thinking out loud, you allow the interviewer to see your logical train of thought so that they can help you when you become stuck.

4) **Practice.** There is no substitute for hard work. Prepare answers for most of the common questions that come up – see later sections of this book – and arrange as many practice interviews as you can. The myth that you cannot prepare for interviews is just that – a myth!

STRUCTURE OF THE INTERVIEW

The IM interview will take place over the course of three different stations, each lasting approximately 10 to 15 minutes in length. The main topics covered by each station are your portfolio and suitability for IM, a clinical scenario and communication skills station, and a medical ethics and professionalism station.

When you arrive for the interview, you will enter a room with a number of other applicants. Your Eligibility Folder and Evidence Portfolio will be taken from you and be checked by the administrators on the front desk. They will go through your Eligibility Folder, and remove the copies that they need. You will then sign in, and take a seat waiting for your interview slot. This is the most difficult part of the interview, especially if the previous group is running late (as tends to happen). Try to stay focused on yourself and why you are there – often running through your answers in your head can help. Generally speaking, it is best to avoid talking to the other candidates about the application or interview. You do not want to lose confidence talking to someone who is bragging about their high score, and equally you don't want to enter a false sense of security that may reduce your sharpness during the interview.

You will then be called into your interview circuit as a group of 3 – one applicant per station – and you will rotate through each station in the circuit. Therefore, you are not guaranteed to start at any particular station, so don't go in expecting to sit the stations in a set order.

You will be given 5 minutes of reading time prior to being called into the interview room. This is of most relevance to the Clinical Scenario and Ethical Scenario stations. Use this time to familiarise yourself with the case, and to start thinking about what you would do if you were in the situation described by the scenario. After all, that is what you are going to be asked about when you are called into the interview.

Finally, you will be called in, and will go through a series of questions about each station. Once you have finished in that station, you will take a seat outside and wait to move round in the circuit, and the process repeats itself until all three stations are finished.

Interview Scoring: A Recap

As we mentioned in Chapter 3 (The Application & Scoring), you are scored by two different interviewers on a scale of 1 through 5 in two different areas, which vary based on the particular station. These categories are shown below:

Station	Scoring Areas
Station 1	Evidence
	Suitability for IM
Station 2	Clinical Scenario
	Communication Skills
Station 3	Ethical Scenario
	Professionalism and Governance

Therefore, each interview station is actually scoring you on two different characteristics. In Station 1, it is difficult to separate the two scoring areas as they are so closely intertwined. However, in the other two areas, there will be different aspects of each scenario or even two different scenarios within each station, and thus you need to be able to score marks for both categories. We will turn to a discussion of each station in turn, covering first the different things that the interviewers are looking for, and then turning to specific questions or scenarios that often come up during the exam.

STATION 1: THE PORTFOLIO

The first station of the interview that we will discuss in detail is the portfolio station. If you have followed the steps detailed in Chapter 5 and prepared an organised portfolio then this station should be quite enjoyable for you – as the interviewers already have all the answers they need in front of them, and it's just up to you to fill in the blanks!

As we mentioned earlier, when you arrive for the interview your portfolio will be taken from you and given to the interviewers. They will then look through it prior to you being called into the room. The interview itself will consist of a series of questions about why you want to do IM, your career aims and ambitions, and your portfolio and background. This station will last for varying lengths of time depending on your chosen deanery, but expect this to last approximately 10 minutes. As you can see, this is a relatively short amount of time, and so preparing your answers in advance is one of the keys to success.

Sample Questions

We will now turn to a range of sample questions, which are likely to appear in your interview. We will discuss both bad and good responses to each question, analyse why these answers are good or bad respectively, and then provide a discussion of each of the questions. There are different ways of reading through this chapter: I would recommend that you look at the question, and then cover the page and attempt to think or write down how you would answer it. You should then refer back to the text to see how your answer matches the principles illustrated in our examples and advice, and see if there is any way that you can improve on the answer you wrote down.

1) Why do you want to apply for Internal Medicine?

This is a common question to begin the portfolio station with. The easy thing for you here is that you have essentially already written this answer in the online application as part of the 'commitment to specialty' answer. You should feel free to use this as the foundation of your response.

An excellent response will show strong enthusiasm for medicine, and will show that you know how IM will fit in towards your future career plans.

A Bad Response:

I want to do IM because I know that I don't want to be a surgeon. During my placement in F2, I liked the work in A&E overall, but I don't like the working patterns associated with A&E. I think, therefore, that IM will give me a good balance of seeing acute medical conditions, but will allow me to train in a specialty that gives me more of the work-life balance that I was looking for.

Response Analysis:

Don't give negative reasons. You need to show the interviewers that this is your top job choice, and you are determined to achieve a place within IM. It is important to be enthusiastic at all times, and focusing on negative reasons means this comes across as a negative answer.

Working patterns in IM can be tough with the on call schedule – this answer makes the candidate sound like they don't like hard work!

A Good Response:

My career aspirations are to be a top Gastroenterologist. As you can see from section 7 of my portfolio, I have performed a QI project within this specialty looking at rates of variceal re-bleeding, and have given several presentations related to Gastroenterology during my time at medical school. I know that IM will provide me with an excellent foundation for future registrar training in Gastroenterology, and therefore I am extremely excited about the prospect of continuing my medical training in depth as part of IM.

Response Analysis:

This answer shows that the candidate has a career plan and goals, and is determined to achieve them. It shows that they have been thinking about this for quite a while, as they have been able to tailor their application towards the specific specialty that they are interested. They are enthusiastic about the future prospects as working as a Gastroenterologist, and know that IM is the path into this specialty.

Overall:

This is an easy question to answer, and is one that you should expect to come up in your interview. Prepare in advance, using the commitment to specialty question in your application as a guide. You don't have to deliver a long argument about why IM is the right job for you – showing the examiners strong reasons about why you want to do IM in a succinct and organised manner will be very impressive to them.

2) Why do you want to train in this specific Deanery?

Do your research about where you are applying beforehand! What are the particular strengths? How do they match your career aspirations?

This question can let you score some easy points with examiners. It does not take a lot of work – if you don't know already – to find out the strengths of a particular deanery or hospital that you want to work in. By doing this research, you are able to convey to the interviewer that you are taking an active role in your career planning.

A Bad Response:

I really like London as a place to live. It allows me to engage in a wide range of activities that let me balance appropriately my work-life balance. This lets me decompress and relax after work, and so I think this makes me a better doctor. In addition, my long-term friends are applying to train here and so I want to be able to continue to maintain my important friendships with them.

The number of different clinical opportunities available in London is incredible, and would let me get experience in a diverse number of different specialties before making the decision as to which specialty I want to pursue in my career.

Response Analysis:

This answer does provide a number of good reasons for applying to a specific area. However, this response leads with several personal reasons for the applicant choosing this particular deanery. Whilst personal reasons can be valid in this type of answer, I certainly would not lead with them. It is important to lead with several professional reasons to show your seriousness as an applicant.

There is absolutely no problem with informing the examiners that you are not 100% sure what specialty you want to apply to in future. That is part of the function of IM: to let you gain further experience in a variety of specialties. However, you should at least demonstrate that the particular place you are applying for entry to will allow you to make progress in your career planning. Showing the interviewers that you know that there are hospitals, known for certain specialties, that you want to work in tells them that you have done your research as to why a particular deanery would help you make your decisions about what specialty to apply for.

A Good Response:

My career goal is to be a consultant Neurologist. I believe this deanery is an excellent place to be a Neurologist as the clinical facilities in this location are second to none. For example, the Royal hospital acts as a quaternary centre for a number of challenging Neurological presentations, and therefore I will be able to expand my horizons by seeing a wide variety of patients that I may not get to see elsewhere. This will provide me with excellent experience prior to my registrar training.

During my medical student elective, I was able to spend a short amount of time within the Neurology department at the Royal hospital. I have realised that this is an environment that I would love to work in. In addition, I completed one Quality Improvement project on anti-epileptic drug prescription, and have a second project in the planning stages with two of the consultants in the department.

I have also spoken with some of the trainees in years above me, and they felt that the teaching provided within this deanery is very good for current CMTs, with a number of deanery-wide teaching days on a variety of different medical problems.

Response Analysis:

This is a good answer for a number of reasons. It shows that the candidate has a specific career in mind, and is motivated to achieve this. It shows that they have considered where they would like to do this, and how this particular deanery matches in with both their previous experience and future goals. It demonstrates that the candidate has a relationship with the department and is likely to be successful in getting future projects going. Finally, it shows that the candidate has done their own research to hear about what previous trainees have felt about this deanery, which again shows a strong commitment to this specific area.

Overall:

This question requires a bit of a balance. It is important to show that the reasons for applying to a specific deanery were made because the candidate feels that this particular deanery is in a good position to be able to help achieve their career goals. A good way is to look at the various strengths of the area, and to see which of these strengths match your ambitions.

The balance comes in discussing personal reasons that have influenced your decision. Whilst these reasons are of course completely valid and make up an important part of your decision, it can come across as an unprofessional decision based on how you phrase it. If it were me, I would just avoid discussing personal reasons in this question. However, it really depends on your individual circumstances. If you feel that that it comes across as a sensible reason that will improve your concentration and motivation as a doctor – for example, your children are in local schools, then it would certainly come across as an important and genuine influencer of your decision.

3) What is your biggest achievement on your CV?

Think carefully about your CV prior to the interview. This is one of the first things the interviewers will see when they open your portfolio, and their eyes will be drawn to any sections that stand out. Therefore, when designing your CV, have this in mind so that things you are most proud of stand out.

A Bad Response:

There are many things in my CV that I am proud of. I am proud of the intercalated degree that I performed, and am proud of the high grades I received at the end of this year. I am proud of the distinction that I gained during my clinical training. I am also proud of the presentation that I gave last year at a regional conference detailing the findings of my Quality Improvement project on venous thromboembolism prophylaxis. Of all of these achievements, I am most proud of my dissertation as this was something I worked extremely hard for.

Response Analysis:

Whilst this technically does answer the question, it essentially comes of as reading a list. It can be a good tactic to briefly highlight several things that that you are proud of that you may not get to mention before focusing on one in particular, but this answer doesn't really come to give a detailed discussion on one of these achievements. The answer also does not show how this achievement makes them a better applicant for IM.

A Good Response:

There are several things that I am proud of on my CV, including my First Class Degree, my QI project, and my strong laboratory experience. What I am most proud of, however, the prize I won at a national junior doctor conference for my QI project that I performed last year. I investigated the rates of venous thromboembolism prophylaxis that were prescribed in my first F1 rotation. I identified that this was well below target, and came up with several suggestions to improve this, including a box on each admission document that had to be filled in.

This year, I performed a re-audit and showed that the rate of prophylaxis being prescribed has significantly increased. We will await findings to see if this has resulted in a drop in VTE events. I am very proud of this work because I designed the project and interventions myself, and I feel that I have been able to make a difference in the care of a large number of patients – and that is what I studied medicine to do.

This has taught me how to carry out a successful QI project, and the importance that all doctors engage in this activity to improve patient safety. I will look forward to performing further during my career.

Response Analysis:

The applicant was able to list 3 impressive achievements, but then quickly zero in on one achievement to avoid the ire of the interviewers. They then explained well what the achievement was, the impact that it has made on both patients and the applicant themselves, and what they have learned going forwards.

Overall:

This is a good opportunity to show of a significant achievement of yours that you may not get to discuss with the interviewers otherwise. Each individual applicant will have a number of different achievements that they can draw on, but the core principles remain the same. Discuss the achievement, what you have learned from it, and how it makes you a better doctor.

4) What are you most proud of since starting work as a doctor?

This is similar to the last question, except that it narrows down the time window to the prior year and a half or so. This therefore demands that the applicant has continued to strive to be an engaged trainee. Don't get concerned thinking that you haven't done much over the Foundation Programme to date – they are extremely difficult years! – but every applicant will have made themselves proud through any number of achievements.

A Bad Response:
I think that I am most proud of the teaching that I gave to medical students on the ward during my Care of the Elderly rotation. I taught the students how to examine a number of different systems, and they were all grateful to be shown how to do this. They all received good feedback in their OSCE, and so I felt I had made a difference in their training. This is something I am very proud of.

Response Analysis:
This isn't a terrible answer by any means. Teaching is an important part of any medical career, and it is good to feel proud of helping your students achieve good grades. However, all doctors are expected to engage in training the next generation of doctors, and this answer, whilst perfectly functional, does not come across as enthusiastic or suggest that the achievement really stands out in one way or the other.

A Good Response:
I organised a 5-session clinical skills course for medical students rotating through my Care of the Elderly block. I taught them how to examine the cardiovascular, respiratory, abdominal, cranial nerves and neurological systems. I organised an attendance register, and those that successfully attended all sessions received a certificate afterwards.

I used the feedback from my first sessions to update my subsequent ones so that they suited the students' requirements. All of the students within my group then passed their OSCEs easily. I ran the course again during my next block for a different set of students. I was then contacted by the University who explained they were grateful for my involvement in the teaching of their students, who had been providing good feedback about my course.

I am proud of this achievement because I achieved recognition for a course of my own design that resulted in better education for medical students. I was recognised by the University for this, and I will therefore continue to develop this course, getting other foundation trainees to continue to deliver it. It convinced me to perform a higher education degree during my training at some point.

Response Analysis:
This answer does illustrate another example of post-graduate teaching, but shows that the candidate has significant enthusiasm about the course that they designed, and pride for the recognition they received about it. They discussed how it will influence their future career.

Overall:
There are many different topics that could be the subject of your answer within this question – teaching, QI projects, presentations, case-reports or other publications... The key is to show the examiners that you are proud of this achievement, and how it has led to your continued professional development.

5) What is your biggest weakness?

This question often catches candidates out. A careful balance needs to be struck between not coming across as arrogant and demonstrating a dangerous lack of insight (nobody is perfect!). It is also important not to identify a weakness that may make the examiners worry about your safety as a doctor – therefore do not give an answer that can be interpreted as medically negligent. The answer needs to identify a weakness and then demonstrate how you are attempting to rectify this.

Avoid the urge to give an answer that is not really a weakness, e.g. "I'm a perfectionist", as a more profound degree of self-criticism will be appreciated more. Instead, by simply changing the phrasing and customising it to yourself, you can say something very similar, e.g. *"my time management can be a weakness, often because I take on too many projects at the same time"*. You would need to develop this by showing what you've learnt from reflecting on your weakness, e.g. *"...so when I am working on a project, I ensure that I know exactly what the timeline is to completion before taking on more work."*.

Showing humility when answering a question such as this is a good way to make you appeal to the interviewer as a person. Some candidates may be tempted to answer this with a joke, however, this is not advisable as it is a very important question for medics.

A Bad Response:
My biggest weakness is that I'm sometimes quite arrogant. I've always been very successful at most of the things I try and do and so have an awful lot of self-belief. I rarely feel the need to ask for help as I know that I will likely be OK without it. When I fail at something, I get very angry with myself and will often feel down for several days afterwards.

Response Analysis:
This is a dangerous response. Many applicants will indeed be very good at lots of things; however, saying that this has made them arrogant is not good. The candidate states that they rarely seek help for things and have an innate belief that they will be good at anything they turn their hand to. It is not possible to be good at everything from the offset, and knowing when to ask for more senior help is an absolutely critical part of being a doctor. In medicine, it's not just that your ego will be bruised if you fail, but a patient's health may be severely affected.

A Good Response:
I consider myself a natural leader and so my instinct in many situations is quite often to lead the team and exert my authority in coordinating others. However, I appreciate that quite often during my medical career I will not be the most appropriate individual to lead a team. Therefore, I'm working really hard on my skills in working effectively within a team and not necessarily as the leader. In order to improve on this, I've paid significant attention to the (good) feedback that I received during my Team Based Assessments, looking at specific areas of my team working skills that I can improve. I have also attended a course that illustrated several different types of personality within teams, and how to ensure your personality adapts to the specific team environment. The work I have done has let me become a much more successful member of the medical teams I have been a part of throughout my time as a doctor so far.

Response Analysis:
This candidate identifies a valid weakness that, if too extreme, would be a problem in medical practice. However, crucially the candidate has demonstrated insight into this problem and how this could be an issue as a doctor. Impressively, they've even shown that they are being pro-active in trying to address this weakness.

Overall:
Medical practice is quite rightly very keen on quality control and ensuring best practice. Therefore, it is essential that those that practise medicine have sufficient insight to identify where they are struggling and when to ask for help. Indeed, many important decisions about patient care are made during multidisciplinary team meetings, and all doctors need to be able to be successful and involved members of these teams. A good doctor will identify their flaws and adjust these so as to prevent the quality of patient care being affected.

6) What do you find the most stressful thing about being a doctor?

Honesty is important in this question. Think about some of the most stressful times that you have experienced as a junior doctor in your career – there clearly will be more than a few of these! – and reflect on them to think of experiences that were particularly impactful on you. This will form the basis for a variety of the different types of question that you will get in the interview: from stressful circumstances, to those demonstrating good communication skills, and to those that were the most rewarding.

A Bad Response:

I find it most stressful when there are multiple demands for my time. For example, I can get quite worked up when I am on call at night and have 3 patients in different parts of the hospital that are all really sick and that I need to see to as soon as possible. I feel like I am prone to panicking in this situation, but always manage to calm myself down and then see the sickest patient first, making my way through each patient one by one. I hope that I will be able to develop my skills further in IM so I can see patients like this much faster.

Response Analysis:

This clearly is a valid stressor that most, if not all, of us will have experienced on numerous occasions. The issue with this answer, however, is that it is too negative and suggests that the applicant is really struggling with these occasions. Some of the words used may be cause for concern on the part of the interviewer. The answer does suggest the importance of stratifying patients so the sickest are seen first, but it fails to mention escalation to seniors or other team members when support is needed, which would be the most important thing for patient safety. You must not give answers that suggest there may be a risk to patient safety by your actions.

A Good Response:

Medicine can be a very stressful profession, and it is important to find mechanisms of coping with this stress.

One of the things I find most stressful about medicine are the occasions, often when on call, when there are more things to do than time allows. This can be particularly stressful when there are multiple sick patients to see at the same time, and I worry about leaving patients that I can't see immediately in an unsafe condition.

To combat this I have developed several techniques. I have improved my information gathering and consultation that I do over the phone with the nurses – I get up to date observations on patients, and am able to assess the urgency of the situation. When there are multiple patients to see I write a list of their details and quickly assess which are the most urgent to get to, and then work through my list in order. If I feel two must be seen urgently, then I call the other members of the on call team to ask their help, which allows me to maintain patient safety.

When I get home, I ensure that I have time to relax and read a book before bed. This lets me to rest my mind and ensures that I am able recharge prior to my next shift, which makes me a more efficient, and safer, doctor.

Response Analysis:

This answer shows a good deal of insight, and shows that the candidate has really thought about what makes them stressed about their job. Having multiple unwell patients is a common concern. However, despite that, the candidate has been able to make the answer unique to them by discussing their individual concerns, tactics to alleviate the stress in the situation, and about how they have learned to cope with this stress.

Overall:

You may be noticing a theme at this stage. One of the critical things in this interview – and indeed interviews in general – is to relate the experiences you are describing to attributes required for the job you are applying to. Here, the successful candidate is able to discuss genuinely stressful experiences, and then discuss how they have reflected and learned from these circumstances, and how that in turn has made them a better candidate for the job. If you can do the same, then the interviewers will be impressed with the thought that has gone into your answer.

7) What teaching experience have you had in your Foundation Years?

This is another question where you have done a significant amount of work prior to the interview about. There is an entire section about teaching in your application and portfolio, and therefore you should discuss the most impressive or in-depth teaching that you have done as part of this. You can impress the examiners with discussions around how you have thought about continuing this teaching going forward into IM.

A Bad Response:

When I was a foundation year doctor, I did some clinical examination skills teaching for medical students. I showed them how to examine the abdominal and respiratory systems as preparation for their OSCE examinations. I was able to find patients on my ward with good clinical signs for them to examine. They told me afterwards that they thought the teaching was extremely useful, and therefore I have continued to offer this teaching to other medical students.

Response Analysis:

This is a good example of teaching. It does show that the candidate put some thought into finding appropriate patients for their students. However, it doesn't reflect on feedback received in any meaningful way, and doesn't demonstrate why they think teaching is an important part of any clinical career.

A Good Response:

Teaching is a responsibility of qualified doctors to ensure future doctors are trained to the highest quality standards. I designed a series of clinical skills teaching sessions for final year medical students in my Trust. This formed an 'examination skills course', and I was able to issue certificates to the students following the successful completion of this course.

I taught my students how to perform cardiovascular, respiratory and abdominal examinations. I collected feedback forms from the students after each session. I saw that after the first session the students felt that seeing more patients with clinical signs would be useful, and therefore before subsequent sessions I made a concerted effort to find at least 2 patients that would demonstrate useful signs in the relevant system. Judging by the feedback, this change was extremely well received by the students. From this experience I learned that I really enjoy teaching, and saw first-hand the importance of obtaining feedback following teaching. Using the sessions I designed, I would like to continue this course with future medical students on the wards during IM.

Response Analysis:

This is a good answer for a number of reasons. It shows the candidate engaged with deliberate planning of what sessions they were going to provide to their students. It showed that they organised a formal course so that their students would have something tangible to show for their achievements. It also demonstrates that the candidate knows the importance of, and was receptive to, feedback following the sessions. Finally, they show that they know the importance of teaching within the medical profession, and have a desire to continue this during their future career.

Overall:

Teaching is one of the responsibilities of qualified clinicians. Demonstrating that you have engaged in teaching from an early stage is important to the interviewers, because you will frequently be the one providing the ward based teaching to medical students during IM. Showing that you are actively engaged in the planning and delivery of teaching demonstrates a responsibility towards your privileged post, and this will greatly impress the interviewers.

8) When have you had to show good leadership skills?

Being an effective leader is important in a wide range of medical situations: from the acute decisions regarding patient care during a cardiac arrest, all the way to the high-level managerial decisions that many hospital consultants get involved with. A good leader has exceptional communications skills, listens to each member of the team, and is able to make appropriate decisions when required. They must also take ownership of the decisions they make, both during good and bad outcomes.

A Bad Response:
I am at a very junior stage of my career and so it is difficult to think of many circumstances when I have shown leadership skills. However, I did act as the local British Medical Association representative for my trust, and so obtained good leadership skills as a result of my role. I attended and organised several meetings during my time in this role, and improved my organisational skills as a result.

Response Analysis:
Even though it is true that IM applicants are at a relatively junior stage, it is not correct that they have little leadership experience. This experience may include leadership roles in varying clubs within university, teaching positions held, roles taken during volunteering/the elective, local BMA representative positions held, and a huge number of other opportunities besides. Therefore, you must have an answer planned that illustrates a leadership experience example, and should be able to discuss your role, what you learned, and how this prepares you to be a future leader within medicine.

A Good Response:
Leadership skills are an essential part of being a good doctor. They allow good communication within a team, and are essential when trying to ensure that a team is running to the fullest of its potential. I served on our local BMA representative team for our trust and took on a leadership role within this team. After discussing the work we needed to accomplish with the other team members, I delegated tasks according to individual team members' strengths, and made decisions regarding where our priorities for our ambitions had to lie. After coordinating our different strategies, we were able to successfully negotiate a change in the F1 medical on call rota that allowed it to maintain patient safety, and also enabled the junior doctors on the rota to be able to use their full annual leave allocation. Throughout this experience, I learned the important requirements of being a leader: good communication skills within the team, the ability to make decisions when required and take responsibility for their outcomes, and the requirement for hard work such that I could lead by example.

Response Analysis:
This answer shows much more insight into the requirements of a good leader in the medical profession, and why leadership skills are important. It gives a clear example of a time when the candidate demonstrated leadership skills, the changes they were able to bring about, and the lessons they learned from this experience.

Overall:
This is another question that is very likely to come up, and unless you have prepared in advance, can be difficult to come up with a good example on the spot. The key requirements are to illustrate a good example of a time you have demonstrated leadership skills, what those skills were, and the outcomes of your experience. If you can relate what you learned to your potential future role – as the consultants of the NHS – then that will impress the interviewers, showing that you know what will be expected of you in the years beyond IM.

9) Why are good management skills required in medicine?

Medicine is an incredible personal profession –you will be interacting with other doctors, nurses and other members of the multidisciplinary team, and, of course, with the patients and their relatives. Management within medicine can take numerous different guises – whether this is managing a team of doctors, managing a ward, being responsible for coordinating a rota, or making decisions regarding funding. Clearly, the interviewers are not expecting you to have performed any of these roles at this stage – and that is why most managerial courses are aimed at registrars and consultants – but demonstrating that you know about management in medicine is another useful bit of evidence for the interviewers that you are engaged actively in career planning.

A Bad Response:

Medical management is about managing people successfully. This will be important during my future career as a medical consultant as I will be in charge of the medical running of my particular ward. I will need to ensure that the juniors beneath me have an appropriate level of supervision, that their work-load is appropriate, and that they are happy with their job. I will also be responsible for investigating how to improve the quality of care we provide on my ward through audit and quality improvement. I plan to develop these skills during my time in IM, and hope that they will prepare me well for my future role as a medical consultant.

Response Analysis:

This answer clearly covers a lot of good points – it makes important points about staff morale, quality improvement, and the running of a ward. However, medical management experience covers many more aspects than just this, and it would be useful to have discussed some previous experience that can illustrate how the candidate may already have some managerial experience.

A Good Response:

Medical management is one of the core pillars of medical consultants' jobs. They may be responsible for the team of doctors under them, be involved in designing and carrying out quality improvement projects to ensure their clinical standards are maintained and improved, and may also be involved in making important decisions regarding the allocation of clinical funding.

I was elected treasurer of my football club during my time in University. This proved to be a fun and useful role for me – not least because I learned some useful techniques for the distribution of our limited funds in our team. I listened to the other club members, and made decisions regarding the funds allocated to renovating our facilities and to providing out kit. The experiences gained here will serve me useful in the future as I take up more of a managerial role within my profession, especially when it comes to making decisions about where to allocate a limited budget. I also plan to engage actively with learning about medical management. I hope to take some online courses and also to attend taught courses to ensure my managerial skills continue to improve.

Response Analysis:

This answer covers many of the important basics when it comes to the role of management in medicine. It gives an excellent example of some prior managerial experience, and how this relates to the future managerial roles that doctors can take within the NHS. The candidate also demonstrates that they realise that there will be further opportunities for developing these skills and that they intend to make the most of this, again emphasising the commitment to specialty and willingness to plan for a successful future as a consultant physician.

Overall:

Questions about medical management often appear in medical interviews, and will come up increasingly as your experience level increases. At the stage of the IM interviews, the interviewers are looking to see that the candidates are aware of the different areas that management skills are important in, and that the candidates know how their training will allow them to develop these skills. If you can communicate this, with any specific managerial examples as an added bonus, then you will come across very well in the interview.

10) Can you tell us about a time when you showed good team-working skills?

One of the most important professional skills required in medicine is the ability to work successfully as a member of a team. IM applicants have a good background when it comes to providing examples for this question because they have worked in teams of doctors over the last year as part of the Foundation Programme. Team-working skills relate to the ability to maximise the performance of a team of people as a member of the team: this may lead to the improvement of patient safety or some other specified team output.

A Bad Response:

I worked as a member of a successful team during my time on a care of the elderly ward at the start of F2. Our team consisted of several other junior doctors, our consultant, and a wide variety of different members of the multidisciplinary team. We were able to successfully divide tasks between us to spread the work load, and I was always willing to help the other members of the team when they had too much work or were dealing with a particularly unwell patient. We also were able to complete two Quality Improvement projects during our time on the ward. Our team was therefore successful in ensuring good patient care.

Response Analysis:

This response does not cover any specific skills that fall under the 'team-working' umbrella. These include, but are not limited to, communication skills, time management skills, organisational skills and leadership skills (though being careful not to overstate this component when discussing your role as a specific team member). Therefore, a good answer should give an example – like the answer above – but should explain how your role within the team illustrates these specific professional skills.

A Good Response:

Working well within a team is an essential skill to possess as a doctor, especially when you consider that we are always work in teams, and those teams are constantly changing (such as when we rotate jobs, or are on call). Therefore, possessing good team-working skills lets me adapt to the different teams that I work with.

One of the most successful teams I worked with was my high-schools Science team – our team won our regional finals and advanced to the national finals. I was able to communicate well with the other members of the team, ensuring everyone had the ability to give their ideas to the group, and I coordinated different members of the team when we had multiple tasks to perform simultaneously. I provided important organisational skills, providing the documentation during the experimental tasks, which allowed our experiments to be more reproducible than other teams. I also provided good time management skills which allowed our team to be one of the few teams to perform all of the tasks within the provided time.

During my first year as a junior doctor I saw how useful these transferrable skills were – I prioritised ward jobs efficiently, and ensured they were completed in a timely manner. I was able to communicate well with different members of the MDT, and successfully arranged investigations or input from other specialties when required.

Response Analysis:

This is a thorough answer that covers the fundamentals of what working in a team means, and what the specific skills required of team working are. Applicants shouldn't feel afraid to give examples that are not directly related to their role as a doctor. In fact, doing so illustrates to the interviewer that you as a candidate know the importance of the transferrable skills that you gained as a member of that team, and can show you in a very good light if you can relate to what you have learned and how it improved your practise as a doctor.

Overall:

Team-working questions are one of the main categories of question to come up during the portfolio station. This is hardly surprising when you consider the fundamental role that team-working plays throughout the entirety of medicine. To ensure you are successful with this, you should familiarise yourself with the core principles of teamwork, and to think examples where you can directly relate these principles to your medical practise.

11) Name some of the difficulties involved in leading a team, how did you make a difference?

Medicine is a profession where you will almost always be working as part of a team. This question is looking for examples in the past when you have worked as a team, but more importantly, the challenges that the team experienced and what you did about those challenges. It is perfectly fine that you had problems working with a team in the past, but the interviewer really wants to see your response to these challenges. This does not have to be related to a medical team (although this can only help the answer) but should show skills desirable in a doctor.

Being a good doctor means more than simply being a good clinician. The interviewer knows that you are capable of leading, but wants you to prove it to them. The way to answer this question is to provide them with a strong example of when you led a team successfully.

A Bad Response:
I do not often lead teams so this question is a little difficult for me. I think I tend to follow the team leader more often, but if no progress is made then I do step up. For example, we were involved in a group presentation and the 'leader' wasn't really leading, so I had a discussion with the other members and it was decided that I should become the leader for this presentation. I was quite uncomfortable with the whole situation but I didn't really have a choice. We managed to get the presentation together after I became the team leader. In this way, I think I did do a good job of leading the team.

Response Analysis:
This answer lacks confidence and assertiveness. These are skills that good leaders should demonstrate when leading their teams. The candidate perhaps did not use the best example of leading from the front as they had not volunteered to be the leader but were coerced into the position. The answer could have been improved by expanding further on how the candidate thinks they did as a leader; did they motivate their peers after morale was low, did they assigns tasks to people?

A Good Response:
I have developed my teamwork skills over my years at school but this has not been without challenges. I really love tic-tac-toe so I quickly joined my school club in Year 9; however, I was disappointed that the club was not running enough events so I met with the president to discuss my concerns and she offered me a position on the executive committee. When working on the committee to organise an interschool tic-tac-toe competition, I had trouble dealing with the treasurer who was not responding to my emails. I arranged a meeting with him and found out that he was having family problems. I offered to help him with his current situation and further suggested that he talk to our college counsellor. I had to delay some of the payments for the event but it all got sorted after one week. I found that by talking to unresponsive members of the team, the real issue could be understood and this helped to build team unity.

Response Analysis:
This response is significantly better than the first, although, note the similarities in much of the content. The first main difference is the person concentrates on what they did within a team rather than talking about how they led a team. The person also brings in a specific challenge that they faced in this team as well as a suitable way of dealing with the challenge (they also showed empathy in this response).

Overall:
This question may throw a few people because it involves talking about a weakness or challenge, but do not be fooled. You should show your strengths by showing how you dealt with a particular challenge. This will be a common theme in questions that ask about challenges that you faced in the past. The main part of this question lies with how you worked within a team to create a positive impact; any challenges that you faced and how you dealt with them also increase the maturity of the response.

12) What are your biggest strengths?

This is a good question to be able to show off what you are proud of within your application, but requires a balance to ensure that you don't come across as arrogant. Consider that the interviewers are looking for their future trainees: they want to know they will be working with successful yet humble applicants.

In addition, when planning this answer, don't forget what job you are applying for. IM is a demanding and rewarding programme, and requires good organisational, time management and communication skills. Therefore, consider the elements that are required of a successful IM doctor, and relate your answers to them. Finally, your answer will always have more impact if you give a specific example illustrating your example.

A Bad Response:
I feel that I make a very good applicant for IM because I fulfil the main requirements of a IM doctor as laid out in the personal specifications: I am hard-working and resilient, and I have good communication skills. In addition, I have good leadership, time management and organisational skills. These strengths make me a good applicant for IM, and will stand me in good stead for my medical career post-IM.

Response Analysis:
This answer superficially covers a lot of the important points for IM applicants. However, it seems as if the applicant is just reciting the personal specifications. What applicant for any higher medical training programme isn't going to say that they have these skills? Therefore, ensure that you give an overview of your skills, but don't forget to focus on specific samples that make you come across as more personable.

A Good Response:
I believe I have several strengths that would improve my ability to be a successful IM doctor. Communication is one of the key components of being a good doctor. I have good communication skills, as evidenced by the fact that my communication skills teacher in medical school invited me to be an instructor for younger students.

I also am a very resilient person. I had a very difficult start to the Foundation Programme as I was in a very demanding job confounded by understaffing, and came across several clinical situations where I felt out of my depth. I was able to remain calm, escalate where required, and kept my patients safe throughout this time. I was very stressed outside of work with this, though. I spoke with my educational supervisor and reflected on these events. I realised that I did what was necessary to maintain patient safety, and this understanding helped me keep perspective when I feel under stress at work.

Finally, I think that organisation is a key component of being successful in IM, especially when it comes to balancing the ward work, on call rota, portfolio requirements and exams. I have been involved in two QI projects and a clinical research project throughout my time in the Foundation Programme, and have therefore developed my organisational skills in a way that will allow me to succeed within IM.

Response Analysis:
This is a good answer for a number of reasons – it discusses several key strengths required of doctors in general, and provides specific examples for each of these. This lets the interviewers gain more of an insight into the applicant's background. In addition, the strengths mentioned focus in on the requirements for success in the IM programme, which in turn informs the interviewers that the applicant has given extensive thought into how these requirements match their strengths as a doctor.

Overall:
Remember, the interviewers are looking at the applicants as potential trainees and colleagues of theirs, and so they want to know more about you and how your past experiences have led you to developing the strengths that you discuss. Therefore, providing context for the examples you mention can be a very powerful tool in demonstrating your suitability for IM.

13) Where do you want to be in five years time?

This is another question that is important to prepare in advance. It looks extremely poor if you arrive at interview and state that you want to do IM because you want a career in 'X', but are unable to exactly explain what the career trajectory in this specialty would look like. Prior to the interview, I would prepare answers for '5 years', '10 years', and '15 years'.

A Bad Response:

I have yet to confirm exactly what specialty I intend to pursue in my future career, though at this early stage I am leaning towards Respiratory medicine. Therefore, I think that in 5 years I will be a specialty trainee in respiratory medicine. I also think that I would like to move back to my home in Newcastle so I think I will apply there for specialty training.

Response Analysis:

While this does show that you at least know that becoming a registrar is the step after core medical training, it doesn't give any more insight other than that. It is important to show you have considered all of the different requirements for progression, and that you know how to meet these.

It also doesn't come across as overly enthusiastic – and would be better to show more commitment to your specialty of choice at this stage. Mentioning that you think Respiratory medicine is something you are really excited about and is what you want to apply in does not commit you at this stage. But it gives a much more committed impression to your interviewers.

Finally, whilst mentioning personal reasons for making certain choices isn't necessarily a 'mustn't do', I would suggest that unless you think it makes a very useful argument and sounds professional, then I would avoid mentioning it.

A Good Response:

In 5 years I plan to have a training number and be engaged in Neurology specialty training. I plan to gain my full MRCP qualification over the next two years, and will use some of my study leave allowance, and Quality Improvement projects, to gain further specialty experience within Neurology.

I also plan to be working towards performing a higher research degree (I'm not sure at this stage if this will be a PhD or an MD). Something I find fascinating is the study of how nerves regenerate, and I feel that I would like to take this further by performing a project oriented around this topic.

Response Analysis:

This answer shows a clear idea of what the candidate wants to do for a future career. It shows that the candidate knows what the requirements are for entering specialty training (exam requirements, and specialty experience, for example). It shows that the candidate is thinking about other professional aspirations at this early stage, which confirms to the interviewers that the candidate is actively engaged in career planning.

Overall:

The interviewers want to know that the trainees that they appoint to the programme are motivated individuals who have taken the time to think about what career they want to have in future. This is not a difficult task to accomplish – it is easy to find out what requirements for entry to different specialties are, what different opportunities are available in each, and to explain what makes you excited by these choices. If you can communicate this to the interviewers then they will have no choice but to be impressed with your answer.

14) Have you had any clinical experiences where you have shown good communication skills?

This is a question that asks you to look at your previous experience, identify a challenging time that required you to be able to communicate well, and show how this led to a resolution/good result in the particular situation. It is not a question asking you to list various difficult discussions with relatives, or to talk about how you also have good organisational skills. It is about communication, and it is important that you stick to this topic when answering. Before answering, it is useful to think about what having good communication skills actually means, and why it is important in your choice of training programme, IM.

A Bad Response:

During my time on the Elderly Care ward, I had a number of difficult communication discussions with patients. I specifically recall a time when we had to inform a family that a patient with dementia was not responding to any treatment we were trying, and that the patient was now in the terminal stages of their disease.

The patient's family were distressed to hear this, and were surprised to use the word 'terminal' in relation to dementia – they thought their relative would continue to live for years to come. I explained how the end stages of dementia can be very difficult to manage, and if a patient stops engaging that there is very little that we can do clinically to improve this. The family were understanding of this, and were able to come to terms with their relative's disease. They thanked me for their time.

Response Analysis:

Whilst at first glance this response doesn't seem particularly bad. However, it doesn't really set the scene with regards to the importance of good communication skills, which doesn't show the interviewers that they have a great deal of insight into this. It also does not state what the candidate learned from this experience, and this is important as reflective practice is a key to improving our abilities as clinicians.

A Good Response:

Good communication skills are required in any medical specialty. I found that I used my communication skills every day when I was a junior doctor, including in difficult patient and relative discussions, discussions with other colleagues in the hospital, and within my ward team.

One time in particular makes me think positively on my previous communication skills experiences. I had a patient on my ward who had developed rather suddenly end-stage kidney disease. The patient had had a relative undergo dialysis, and he had made the decision rather early on that he did not want to receive this treatment, fully understanding that he may die as a result.

His family found this very difficult to understand, and his son rather angrily asked to speak to me. He said that I was clearly not doing my job appropriately if I couldn't convince his father to have the life-saving treatment. I was able to de-escalate the situation by apologising for any confusion, and by asking the patient to talk fully through his concerns. I also brought the son a cup of tea prior to our discussion. I then turned to discussion about mental capacity and how it is entirely within a patient's rights to refuse life-saving treatment if they so choose.

The son understood this but it didn't solve his concerns. I explained that his father felt dialysis had robbed his relative of a lot of his freedom in his last weeks and months alive. We therefore discussed that by not having dialysis, the patient felt that he would be able to have a better quality of life going forward. This was something that the son hadn't considered, and I could see how this had an immediate impact on him. I answered any further questions he had, and brought him back to his father.

I reflected later on this event. I felt that my non-verbal communication skills helped significantly in de-escalating the situation. I realised that I had shown good listening skills in the early stages of the episode, and then had shown an ability to change the angle of discussion when I realised the first approach was not successful. I learned for future practice that using a the medical argument (capacity) in this situation may not be the best initial approach.

Response Analysis:

This is a strong response for several reasons. It shows that the candidate understands that communications skills are not just something to use when talking to patients – it influences every aspect of our day to day practice. In addition, the example given is clear and demonstrates a variety of good verbal and non-verbal techniques used. Finally, the candidate shows they reflected and learned from their experience, which is an essential part of improving our skills as clinicians.

Overall:

It can be easy to fall back to an easy clinical scenario – for example, an aggressive patient that you were able to calm down through your skilled communication techniques. However, this will be a common answer that the interviewers have to listen to, and therefore planning this question in advance with a slightly more unusual story will grab their attention and make you stand out. Let the specific story you give demonstrate important techniques, and show how they worked in the specific situation, and how you learned from what you did afterwards.

15) Tell us about a Quality Improvement project that you have been involved with, describing the aims of the project and whether you were successful in making the desired improvement.

All candidates will have carried out at least one quality improvement project during their Foundation years. Therefore, this answer should be relatively straightforward, but there are ways to score extra points with your answer that you should include.

In recent years, Quality Improvement projects have replaced 'Audits' in terms of the main mechanism by which the NHS wishes to induce change in practice. The general principles of QI projects are relatively similar to Audits, but have a more intentional focus on specifically improving quality, instead of necessarily just measuring certain factors.

QI projects aim to improve healthcare. As defined by the US institute of medicine (www.ahrq.gov/professionals/quality-patient-safety), improving healthcare in general can fall into the following categories:

1. Safety – that the care we provide is always safe
2. Efficacy – the care we provide is effective in improving the lives of our patients
3. Patient-centeredness – the patient is always at the core of the services we provide
4. Timeliness – ensuring the care is delivered on time
5. Efficiency – ensuring efficient processes exist
6. Equitable – consistency for all patients

Therefore, when thinking about a QI project, it should aim to make an improvement in at least one of these aspects, though of course there is significant overlap between them.

SMART (Specific, Measurable, Achievable, Relevant and Time-Bound) aims are the consensus aims in modern QI methodology that show that the investigators have designed a project that is likely to be completed and to come out with results. An example would be: *We aim to reduce the incidence of hospital acquired venous thromboembolism by 90% by August 2019.*

The different stages that are present within QI projects are described below, and form a circle. This model is described as the PDSA model – Planning, Doing, Studying, Acting, and finally returning to planning again.

1. Planning – this is the process by which a project is considered, and the aims of the project are designed. This may mean looking at a specific process that could be made to happen in a more timely manner, for example
2. Doing – this is actually carrying out the suggested changes
3. Studying – this determines whether the desired outcome has been achieved
4. Acting – this then implements the changes

The PDSA (planning, doing, studying, acting and returning to planning) cyclical model is the approach that should underpin each of the changes implemented in the QI project. It is inherently reflective in nature: so in the above example, if we were assessing the incidence of venous thromboembolism each month, then we would perform a PDSA cycle at the end of each month to determine the areas that need to be improved on in the subsequent month.

If you can demonstrate that your QI project was designed to fulfil these criteria, and that you used a PDSA model to assess the impact that you made, then the interviewers will clearly realise that you have a good grasp of the fundamentals of QI, and that you know what is required to run a successful project.

The Audit Cycle

An audit is a systematic investigation into a system to see how it is performing when compared to national guidelines. It allows us to identify any potential problems that might be preventing good medical practice. Once these problems are identified, changes are made to try to resolve them. After a period of time, the audit is repeated again – completing the audit cycle. Hopefully, the changes result in an improvement in healthcare.

Doctors are encouraged to do audits as they can lead to valuable improvements in clinical care. Audits can occur at many levels:

➢ Nationally, e.g. National Stroke Audit
➢ Hospital-Based, e.g. ensuring that all patients are reviewed by a consultant daily
➢ On a ward, e.g. ensuring that all thermometers are correctly calibrated

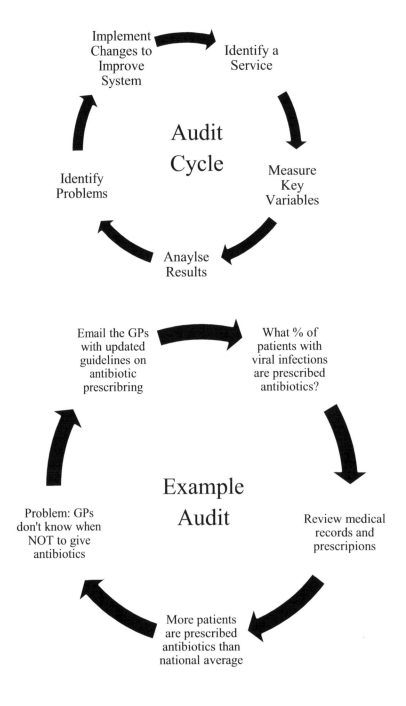

A Bad Response:

I was involved with a QI project in my F1 year that aimed to improve the number of patients receiving appropriate blood cultures during a temperature spike. I discovered that on a number of occasions blood cultures were not being performed in patients who had a spike in their temperature for a number of reasons, including confusion over what the threshold for taking cultures was, and issues surrounding who was 'qualified' to take cultures in our Trust.

I designed posters showing exactly what threshold for the cultures were, and what amount of time from the previous spike meant that the cultures would have to be retaken. I also was able to provide teaching at the hospital-wide teaching sessions for F1/F2s and CMTs. Finally, I discussed with the medical education department about arranging further sessions for ANTT training. These interventions made a significant improvement in the number of patients correctly having blood cultures performed.

Response Analysis:

This, overall, is a reasonable response. However, it does not suggest to the examiner that the candidate knows what quality improvement specifically means, or the fact that it is different to Audit. Additionally, there are a few things that could be changed to improve it further, such as adding some specifics regarding the success of the project, and perhaps some reflection on what the applicant learned for future practise.

A Good Response:

QI projects are becoming the method of choice when it comes to improving the services delivered by the NHS, replacing clinical Audit. Involvement in QI projects is essential for all clinicians as it allows them to reflect on the quality of their care, and to identify ways that it can be improved.

Using the PDSA design model, I was involved with a QI project in my F1 year that aimed to improve the number of patients receiving appropriate blood cultures during a temperature spike. I discovered that in 70% of occasions blood cultures were not being performed in patients who had a spike in their temperature for a number of reasons, including confusion over what the threshold for taking cultures was, and issues surrounding who was 'qualified' to take cultures in our Trust.

I designed posters showing exactly what the thresholds for the cultures were, and what amount of time from the previous spike meant that the cultures would have to be retaken. I also was able to provide teaching at the hospital-wide teaching sessions for F1/F2s. Finally, I discussed with the medical education department about arranging further sessions for ANTT training. These interventions made a significant improvement in the number of patients correctly having blood cultures performed, such that the number is now 85%. This showed me the significant difference that can be made through QI projects.

Response Analysis:

This answer covers the suggestions mentioned above – it gives a clear idea that the applicant understands what QI projects are, and how they performed. It gives a good specific example of a QI project, and clearly states the outcomes of the project. In addition, they state what they learned from this project.

Overall:

QI projects are becoming much more popular with the curriculum organisers of IM and the Foundation Programme. Therefore, a little studying – as described above – will be able to show to the interviewer that you understand that there has been a shift in culture towards QI projects, and that you have a strong grasp of what a QI project is and how it differs from clinical audit. Combining this with knowledge with a good example of a project will see you do very well in this question.

16) Tell me about your interests outside of medicine

This is a good question to be able to link to section 9 of your portfolio. The photographs that you have included allow you to frame your answer, and give you the opportunity to impress your examiners with visual evidence of your hobbies. This isn't a question that asks you to simply list everything that you like to do out of work. You can feel free to list a few things, but should then focus on one or two.

It almost goes without saying, but ensure you do not list activities that can be thought of as unprofessional!

A Bad Response:
I have many hobbies outside of medicine. I like to ski, and have been skiing in the Alps several times in the past few years. I enjoy football, and play in a weekly five aside game. I also serve as the treasurer of this group. These activities allow me to keep fit. I like to read, which I find this a good way to relax. I also enjoy going to the movies with friends, as we all enjoy reviewing new movie releases.

Response Analysis:
Whilst this indicates a well-rounded person who engages in a variety of different activities, it doesn't necessarily suggest that the candidate is particularly enthusiastic (although I am sure they are) about any of these activities. Focusing more on one or two of the activities can demonstrate the sort of motivation and enthusiasm that translates well into a core medical trainee.

A Good Response:
I think maintaining a good work-life balance is crucial, and so I try to lead an active lifestyle that lets me recharge on my days off. I enjoy reading, photography, and working on my website that showcases my photography. However, two of my main interests are skiing and playing football on my local team.
I love skiing, and try to ensure that I go skiing at least once per year. I used to be quite a successful skier, and as a child won several medals in races that I entered. I like to read about new technology in skiing, and so I keep up to date with adaptations that I can make to my boots and skis, such as new bindings. One of the photos on page 50 of my portfolio shows when I went skiing in Colorado.

As I mentioned, I am also a member of my local 5 aside football team. In fact, I am the treasurer for this team, and so as well as keeping fit and providing me with a close group of friends, this provides an opportunity to improve my organisational and management skills. We placed as runners up in a tournament last year, and we are working towards opening new training facilities which will hopefully let us improve even more this year. The photograph on page 51 shows our team receiving our runners-up medal.

Response Analysis:
This is a good answer for a few reasons. It identifies to the interviewers that the candidate understands why having a life outside of medicine is important. It shows that the candidate has a broad range of interests, but zeroes in on a couple of specific interests of theirs. The candidate shows the examiners photos of the events, maintaining their attention, and even discusses the ways that these activities improve their professional skill set.

Overall:
This question allows the candidate to demonstrate real enthusiasm for some genuine interests of theirs. It is very important that this enthusiasm is communicated to the interviewers, as they want to gain a full idea of who you are as a person. Bonus points are certainly available if you can subtly point out how some of your interests improve your transferrable professional skills, such as management experience in the example above. The interviewers want to know that you will a variety of interests that will keep your motivation high, and reduce the risk of burnout, if appointed.

17) What are your top three skills?

This question is assessing your understanding of the skills required in a doctor and your suitability based on those skills. In other words, think of all the different skills you have that enable you to be a good doctor and then pick the three skills that most easily demonstrate these. Ensure that you provide evidence and state how these skills will help you to become a great doctor.

A Bad Response:

I am a brilliantly talented pianist and performed my first solo concert at the age of 15, and so I would have to say that is my number one skill. In aiming for a dream to becoming a concert pianist and a doctor, I have had to remain extremely motivated in order to fit in rehearsal time with my clinical training, I would, therefore, rank my time management as another one of my top skills. I also enjoy musical composition and have received high praise for my work so I would rank my creativity as my third most impressive skill.

Response Analysis:

Whilst this answer demonstrates some remarkable achievements, including skills that are useful as a doctor, it seems to miss the point of the question by solely discussing the candidate's passion for music. It does provide good evidence to back up the candidate's claims, but it should explain why these skills are useful in medicine.

A Good Response:

I would say my top three skills are my communication skills, my interpersonal skills, and my ability to work under pressure. I have demonstrated and developed excellent communication skills through the mentoring system in University in which I provide extra teaching sessions for struggling younger students. This work has helped me to develop my patience, my ability to explain things in a simple way, my ability to understand the concerns of others, and my ability to build a rapport quickly with students who are sometimes nervous and intimidated. These skills are directly transferable to the medical consultation in which doctors must be able to put patients at ease and explain scientific concepts in simple language.

I have always considered myself a people person and show a range of important interpersonal skills. I am a naturally caring person, I take interest in other people and find it easy to be empathetic. I interact confidently with people from lots of different backgrounds. I have further developed these skills during my time on the ward where I enjoy engaging with patients. I have become a better listener in particular from this experience. Again, these skills are vital for a doctor and will help me to treat patients holistically rather than just treating their disease. Finally, through my years on the debating team, I have improved my ability to work under pressure and am confident in making decisions quickly and effectively. This skill is of vital importance when treating patients in an emergency and allows me to keep a cool head in stressful situations.

Response Analysis:

This is an excellent answer that shows a clear understanding of the skills required to be an effective doctor. It promotes the candidate's suitability by providing convincing evidence that the candidate possesses these skills and that they can demonstrate the practical benefits of honing these skills.

Overall:

If you are lucky enough to be asked an open-ended question like this, make sure you take full advantage of it. These types of questions give you huge freedom to display your understanding of the qualities required by a doctor and give you an invaluable opportunity to sell yourself to the interviewer. Make sure you back up everything you say with evidence and continually demonstrate why your skill-set would make you an excellent internal medicine trainee.

18) What do you understand of the Shape of Training changes that are being introduced into medical training?

As we discussed earlier in this book, the Shape of Training changes represent a significant alteration in the way medical training is delivered in the UK. The 2019 IM entry year will be the first time that CMT changes to IM, and becomes a three year training course, and therefore graduates of this programme will be the first to enter the newly designed registrar training course.

Therefore, this question isn't one that was raised in previous years, and it may not be a topic for discussion. However, it would be useful to prepare an answer to this topic should you be asked, as it is always good to show to the interviewers that you know about the changes and how they will affect your training

A Bad Response:

I understand that Shape of Training is a pathway that is designed to modernise the training of medical doctors in the NHS. This pathway aims to increase the number of acute physicians that are able to manage the increasing general medical concerns being seen within the NHS. Core Medical Training will see an increase from 2 years to 3 years, and I believe that is to give us more experience in general medical work as well as to give us more time to prepare our specialty training applications. In the future, it will allow me to train both in my specialty of choice, as well as performing more acute medicine.

Response Analysis:

There is a reasonable understanding of what the changes are going to be here, however the applicant was a little bit light on the details in terms of how CMT is being changes. Equally, the candidate does well to give some reasons as to why the changes have been made, but there are other reasons for this.

A Good Response:

The Shape of Training report represents a significant change in the way postgraduate medical training is to be delivered in the UK. As the population ages, and as patients develop more and more comorbidities, the report feels that an increased number of general physicians are needed to be able to take care of these populations. One of the early ways in which this programme will make changes is to the previous CMT programme. This is being extended from 2 years to 3 years, and is designed to offer up increased exposure to a number of different medical specialties (including in the middle year to high dependency/intensive care medicine).

After CMT, doctors will then apply to specialty training, but the specialties will see a much changed curriculum that means doctors will now spend more time doing general medical work. These changes are designed to update the postgraduate training pathway in a way that hopes to meet the demands of our ageing population.

Response Analysis:

This answer provides a clearer and more focused explanation of the changes and how they will affect the applicant. It shows that the applicant is taking an interest in their future education.

Overall:

This is not a question that has appeared before, for obvious reasons. Therefore, it is unclear exactly how the interviewers will choose to address this topic, if at all. We would recommend that, if asked about the topic, you stick to the facts as illustrated above and reviewed earlier in the book. We would also recommend that you try to avoid focusing on your opinions about the changes, as you do not want to risk offending the interviewers. The internal medicine curriculum brings lots of changes and opportunities, and being positive about this will come across well.

STATION 2: CLINICAL SCENARIO & COMMUNICATION SKILLS

For many, the most daunting station of the IM interview is the medical case scenario. They may feel concerned about the prospect of being asked about a medical condition that they don't know the treatment of, or being asked about a diagnostic test they are not familiar with. You should not be concerned! You have been a doctor for well over a year at this point, and the knowledge you have gained at this time and through medical school is more than enough to see you through this station. The most important thing is to ensure you stick to the structure of what you would do in that specific clinical scenario.

When you arrive outside the Medical Station, you will be given a sheet of paper with an example scenario. You will then be given approximately 5 minutes to read through this, and then be called into the interview. The examiners will ask a range of questions about how you would manage this patient, and then may ask some more in depth questions throughout the station.

This station also focuses on clinical communication skills. Therefore, there will like be a component of the case introduced later (e.g. an angry relative), or sometimes a separate short care, where the examiners will directly ask you questions designed to test your communication skills.

This chapter will cover how to deal with this station, including the important principles to cover, and then turn to a discussion of the common medical presentations that are discussed in the interview. Finally, we will turn to a discussion of the communication skills aspect of the station.

Answering the Medical Scenario

Any clinical scenario can be answered following a set of principles, which ensure patient safety. We discuss these principles now.

A typical case as given in a medical interview will explain your role (IM Doctor), the location (often the Medical Admissions Unit), and a brief history of the patient's presentation. You will then be expected to talk through the scenario with the examiners, who may in turn provide you with further information as you request it (e.g. blood test results). The key to success is to talk the examiners through the case as you would tackle it in real life, making sure to highlight to the examiner when you feel there are times that you need to ensure patient safety.

There are several main areas where you need to highlight this awareness of patient safety. They are:
1. When first seeing the patient, it is important to state you perform a full **ABCDE examination**, and **assess the patient's observations**, so you have an idea if the patient is in immediate danger of acute deterioration
2. If you are concerned with the patient's condition – for example, cannot obtain a pulse – then you should revert to your **Advanced Life Support** knowledge
3. If you have performed the initial assessment and management and are still struggling with the patient's condition, it is essential to **escalate early to a senior** (your Registrar/ITU/Anaesthetist) if you are concerned that the patient needs reviewing by a senior clinician.

A flowchart showing the key things to cover when answering a clinical scenario:

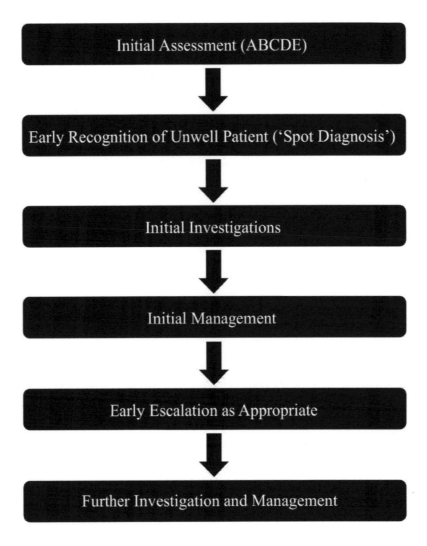

If the patient is clearly unwell and requires admission then you are going to have to tell someone, it doesn't happen magically. The **bed managers** are who you would contact to arrange admission. The interviewers may well want to know that you know what you need to do in order to admit someone from the Medical Assessment Unit or the Outpatient Department.

If you follow the principles as laid out above, and work through the case in a logical manner, then you will be successful in the clinical scenario section of the interview.

Answering the Communication Skills Questions

The communications skills questions may come up as part of the same clinical scenario that the interviewers ask you to work through, or the interviewers may introduce a brief additional scenario that covers the important questions they want to ask. It is often quite obvious during the interview when the focus of the questions switches to discussing communication skills, but you should use every opportunity throughout the clinical scenario to slip in comments that show your verbal and non-verbal communication skills. Examples of this include stating that you would not discuss things with the patient or their relatives in a corridor, but instead would always take them to a 'relatives room' on the ward first. You can mention this before continuing your discussion of the clinical case, and it serves to highlight to the interviewers that you have a highly developed set of communication skills.

There are several common topics that come up during communication skills questioning. We will discuss some of these now.

Mental Capacity & DOLS:

Mental Capacity is one of the most commonly tested ethical scenarios (see the next chapter), but it can come up in briefer form during the clinical scenario. You may be asked how you would assess a patient's capacity, and may be expected to know what to do next should a patient be deemed not to have capacity. You may also have to respect a patient's wishes, should they be deemed to have capacity.

How to assess capacity: in order to assess capacity, a patient must be able to:
1. Understand the information you provide
2. Retain the information
3. Weigh up the information to allow them to come to an informed decision
4. Communicate that decision to you

It is important that you are able to explain in lay terms how you would determine whether a patient does or doesn't have capacity. Broadly speaking, there are two scenarios that would follow this: either the patient has capacity, or they lack it.

In clinical scenarios, if a patient is deemed to **have capacity** but they decline potentially life-saving treatment then it is important that you remember that this decision is entirely down to them, and they have a right to make it. Of course, you must do everything you can to make sure the decision is valid by ensuring the capacity is valid (reflected in your description of how you assess their capacity), but if it is and they make this decision then there is nothing else you can do.

If a patient **lacks capacity**, however, and you need to continue with treatment then you must act in their **best interests**. You must also fill in a **Deprivation of Liberty Safeguard (DOLS)** form – different trusts do this in different ways, so familiarise yourself with your local Trust's policy prior to your interview. We will cover these topics in more detail in the next chapter, but it is important to know for the clinical station should you have a scenario where a capacity decision has to be made.

Aggressive Patients:

This is quite a common addition to the clinical scenario – whether the patient is angry with the care they are receiving, or potentially is suffering from an acute confusional state as a result of their medical illness (particularly look out for this in scenarios involving elderly patients).

There is generally a correct way to answer these questions. We would suggest that you follow this rough guide:
1. Ensure the patient, other patients, staff and yourself are safe before approaching. If this is a concern, then you should ensure the hospital security department is contacted immediately.
2. Oral de-escalation is always the first step in these cases: **never jump straight to sedation.**
3. If the patient is able to calm down with oral communication but remains unsettled, then ensure the patient receives 1:1 nursing, and other supportive measures including something to drink, a settled room for them to stay in, and potentially a discussion with the patient's relatives who may also be able to help
4. Only if all of the above do not work then should you consider pharmaceutical sedation. Again, the first approach must be oral sedation (usually with a benzodiazepine (e.g. 0.5mg Lorazepam)), and discussions with the patient directly may result in them agreeing to take the medication orally
5. If that too fails, and the patient is at significant risk of harming themselves, other patients or staff, then it is suitable to consider intramuscular sedation. Again, **this must be an absolute last resort.**

Following these steps when asked to discuss how to deal with an aggressive patient shows the examiner you know that pharmacological sedation is the last resort, and that you know a variety of verbal and non-verbal de-escalation techniques that would be attempted first. This often leads to successful resolution of these incidents without the requirement for sedation.

Breaking Bad News:

Whilst less likely to occur during an acute medical scenario, breaking bad news is another common topic for interviewers to test candidate's communication skills. They may provide you with, for example, a patient presenting with haemoptysis and weight loss and ask you to talk them through the case to assess your clinical knowledge. They may state that during the initial workup you have noticed a highly suspicious lesion on the chest x ray, and ask you to explain the findings to the patient.

Breaking bad news is definitely a skill. We won't cover the entire principle of breaking bad news here, but will provide some key points to bring up should this topic come up in the interview. Ensure that you respect the patient's **dignity and privacy** at all times: don't tell them in an open bay full of other patients, for example. Ask them if they would like any **relatives** to be present. Try to determine their **baseline knowledge**, asking why you do the chest x ray and if they know what we were investigating for. Ask them if they themselves have any **ideas or concerns** about what might be going on. All of these techniques are serving as **warning shots** for the patient. Explain that there is a suspicious area on the chest x ray (**avoiding medical jargon**), and explain that this has to be investigated urgently as lung cancer until proven otherwise. Advise them that you are **sorry** to have to break this news to them. Ask the patient if they have any **questions** at this stage, and advise that you will provide them with documentation on chest x ray findings, and inform them that they will be seen by other members of the respiratory disciplinary team who will provide more information about further investigation and management options.

Angry Relatives:

This is another common scenario that you will no doubt have witness many times on the ward by now. Knowing how to best manage an upset relative is an important part of being a successful doctor, as it can improve the experience for both the patient and the relative. Therefore, this is another area that the interviewers wish to assess your proficiency in.

There are a few key things to do when informed that a patient's angry relative is on the ward. The first thing that you could do (if it isn't obvious from the history whether the patient knows this relative is in the hospital) is speak with the patient directly and inform them that you believe that their relative is present: and ask them if they would like you to speak with the relative about the details of the patient's case. If the patient declines, then you can not divulge information to the relative.

Greet the relative politely and professionally, and ask them to follow you to a private room where you can have more of a discussion. Ask the relative if they would like a glass of water or a cup of tea. Explain that you are sorry that the relative is upset/angry/concerned with the situation. Ask them to describe the main things that they are upset/angry/concerned with: often the act of talking this through and being listened to is enough to allow the relative to settle. Ensure you illustrate good non-verbal communication skills, engaging in active listening and responding appropriately to the relative's concerns and their cues. Following this discussion, provide enough information as you are allowed (based on whether you have permission to discuss the case) in order to answer their concerns, and provide any suggestions that may improve their situation. Ask them if they feel that this helps with the case, and if there is anything else that they can think of that we should do differently. If they are still upset then explain that they can discuss the case with the Patient Advice and Liaison Service (PALS), and provide them with the appropriate contact information.

This covers some of the most common communication skills topics that come up during the medical interview station. It is not a comprehensive list, but the principles illustrated throughout should provide significant information and techniques for you to follow in a wide range of other communication skills incidents that can come up in this station.

We now turn to an in-depth discussion of the specific clinical scenarios that may come up in the interview, and discuss the important things to cover during your answers. We start with a full example interview, highlighting the keys to success throughout, and

Example Station 2 Interview

Scenario 1:

We will now provide a sample scenario – we will lay this out as if it were the experience of one candidate sitting through this interview station. We will annotate the answer to highlight important components that satisfy the principles as discussed above.

Scenario: You are the IM1 doctor on call, and have been asked to see Miss Price in the Medical Assessment Unit. Miss Price is an 18 year old lady who was found by her boyfriend in her bathroom, deeply asleep. Next to her were an empty half-bottle of vodka, and several empty paracetamol tablets. The boyfriend put them straight in the bin and isn't sure how much she took, but he said he thinks that she didn't take anything else. Her observations on arrival are: HR 73, BP 108/72, Sats 95%, RR 12, Temp 37.1.

Interviewer: *Welcome, please have a seat.*

Candidate: *Thank you, it is nice to meet you.*

Interviewer: *And you. Have you had a chance to look at the scenario? Would you like to talk us through how you would approach this case?*

Candidate: *Yes, I have indeed. Reading the scenario, the first thing I am concerned about is what the clinical situation is at this moment in time: I want to know her GCS and what her observations are to ensure she is stable as it sounds like she is extremely drowsy, and potentially unconscious. As such, on my arrival I would perform a full A through E assessment, and would request an up-to-date set of observations be performed. If I was concerned about the patient's GCS and observations then I would request early input from the anaesthetists and intensive care physicians, as well as my senior.*

Once I established that the patient was in a stable condition, I would attempt to take a full history from the patient, though I realise in this scenario this may be challenging. If she was awake enough to engage with me then important initial questions to ask would be exactly when she took the overdose, how many tablets she took, whether she took anything other than paracetamol (including confirming the volume of alcohol consumed), whether she has any allergies and details about her Past Medical History. I would also want to discuss the episode in more detail, such as what caused her to do this, whether she had planned it or left a note, and whether she is pleased that she is now in hospital, as this will allow for assessment of future risk. If I could not get much of a history from the patient then it would be important to perform an early collateral history.

I would then turn to investigations: I would request an ECG to be performed, and would perform a full set of bloods including FBC, U&Es, LFTs, a clotting screen, and paracetamol and salicylate levels. I would also perform a blood gas. Depending on the results of these investigations I would initiate treatment with N-Acetyl Cysteine, and any further treatment as indicated by the history.

Interviewer: *OK thank you for that, we'll break it down a little and ask some more questions. You performed an initial assessment of the patient's GCS. How would you go about doing this?*

Candidate: *The Glasgow Coma Score is a 15 point score that was designed to assess patients' level of responsiveness post head injury, and therefore is an important way we can characterise the level of consciousness. 6 points are granted for motor responses (for example, whether they can obey commands), 5 points for verbal queues (for example whether they are speaking in full sentences), and 4 points on the patient's eyes (for example whether they are spontaneously open). I am concerned whenever the patient's GCS is not 15, however once the GCS drops by several points I have a very low threshold for escalation.*

Interviewer: *The patient's GCS is 8. What would you do now?*

Candidate: *I would perform an immediate A through E assessment, being particularly concerned about the patient's airway. If they were not maintaining their airway then I would employ different airway adjuncts as required – such as nasopharyngeal airways – until I could secure an airway. If I were not able to secure an airway and the patient were not breathing then I would put out an arrest call.*

Interviewer: *You mentioned that you wanted to perform blood tests, and you mentioned which tests you wanted to perform. What in particular are you looking for in the results?*

Candidate: *The blood tests are important for assessing the level of liver damage. These results include an INR, the creatinine and the arterial pH.*

The paracetamol level will allow me to work out where the patient is on the treatment line in terms of requiring treatment with N-Acetyl Cysteine. Based on the time of onset and paracetamol level measured, I would determine if she would satisfy criteria for treatment. If she did, then I would initiate a NAC infusion, which consists of three bags over a period of about 16 hours.

Interviewer: *What would you do after the infusion?*

Candidate: *I would repeat the blood tests mentioned above, particularly focusing on the U&Es, clotting and arterial pH. I would do this because it is at this stage where if the patient has not responded well then she may consider escalation to intensive care or even with the local liver transplant unit.*

Interviewer: *Here are the results: what would you do in this situation?*

RESULTS:

Hb – 142 g/L	(115 – 165 g/L)
WCC – 7 x10^9/L	(4 – 11 x10^9/L)
Plt – 193 x10^9/L	(150 – 450 x10^9/L)
Na – 138 mmol/L	(133 – 146 mmol/L)
K - 4.8 mmol/L	(3.5 – 5.3 mmol/L)
Ur - 2.5 mmol/L	(2.5 – 7.8 mmol/L)
Cr – 64 mmol/L	(59 – 104 mmol/L)
ALT – 30 iU/L	(<33 iU/L)
ALP – 53 iU/L	(30 – 130 iU/L)
INR - 1.6	
Arterial pH - 7.38	

Candidate: *I would always ensure I followed my local Trust's protocol to make sure I had the values correct, but the main ones I need to confirm are the Creatinine, INR and arterial pH. If the creatinine is greater than 300, if the INR is greater than 6.5, or if the arterial pH is <7.3 then I would immediately call the transplant unit to begin discussions, as well as discuss with my local intensive care department. In addition, the presence of serious hepatic encephalopathy is another indicator of liver damage, and would also prompt discussion with the liver unit. However, in this case I am happy that the bloods are stable and so would proceed with treatment as I mentioned earlier.*

Interviewer: *You mentioned using the local protocols to find out information about treatment guidelines. Where would you find this information?*

Candidate: *I would find this information in the relevant sections of my Trust's intranet.*

Interviewer: *You've told me that the patient's post-NAC bloods are stable. Is there anything else you would do prior to discharging the patient?*

Candidate: *Absolutely. I would ensure that an early referral was placed to the Mental Health Liaison Team, and that the patient was assessed by them prior to her discharge. This, and the answers to the questions I mentioned above, is important in risk-stratifying the patient to determine the risk of her attempting to do this again soon. We would want this to be as low as possible – with arrangements put in place in the community if not – prior to discharge.*

Interviewer: *It is now 6 hours later on in the shift, and the patient's mother accosts you in the corridor, demanding to know why you are keeping her daughter in hospital. How would you handle this situation?*

Candidate: *I would first explain that I understand that she must be concerned, but explain that the corridor is not the best place to have these discussions and that the best thing to do would be to have a private discussion in one of the relatives rooms, if she agreed to it.*

Once we were in this room I would explain that I am unable to give confidential information to the mother without first getting permission from the patient.

Interviewer: *The mum interrupts you here and says she and her daughter have a very understanding and open relationship, and explains that she knows the daughter would want her to know what is going on.*

Candidate: *I would apologise and say that I have to respect the right to confidentiality of my patients, but if she would give me a moment I could potentially ask her daughter if she would be willing for me to discuss her case with her mother. If the daughter gave me permission then I would go through the information with the mother, but if the daughter refused then I would have to apologise to the mother and explain that I am unable to provide her with further information.*

Interviewer: *Later in the shift, about 8 hours into the infusion, the patient becomes quite agitated and disconnects the NAC and is telling the nurses she is insisting on leaving. The nurse runs to you and asks you to speak to the patient. What would you do now?*

Candidate: *I would go speak to the patient and first ask her if there is anything I can provide that will help her to relax, such as a cup of tea. I would try to explain that I understand that it is very frustrated staying in hospital, and I would then ask for her understanding of the situation and why she needed treatment. I would explain that if she did not receive treatment then this was a potentially life-threatening disease which could lead to liver failure, and if turn if not treated then she could die.*

I would explain that she needs to finish the rest of her infusion, and to have the post NAC bloods prior to discharge, because if she doesn't she risks causing permanent damage to her liver, and potentially even death.

Interviewer: *The patient understands this, as she hadn't had this explained to her before. She elects to stay for the end of her treatment. Thank you for your answers. That concludes the clinical station.*

Candidate: *Thank you for the opportunity.*

Analysis: The candidate does well here. They appropriately assess the patient initially, performing GCS and ABCDE assessments in a timely fashion. They correctly investigate and manage the patient, and understand the King's College criteria for liver transplant referral. In addition, the candidate handles well the communication skills section of the station, dealing with the request of the relative and also of the patient's request to leave very professionally.

For the remainder of this chapter we will focus on some of the other common clinical cases that can come up during Station 2. We'll cover these as if the candidate were giving one long answer, and include the key points in their answer, but as you've seen above the interviewers will interrupt and steer the interview as they see fit.

Example Medical Cases

Scenario 2:

A 25 year old male with depression self-presents after taking an overdose of multiple medications. He reports he has taken sertraline, iron supplements and aspirin. He is unsure of the exact quantities because he had alcohol at the same time. You are the IM Stage 1 doctor on the clerking team, and have been asked to see the patient and determine the next steps.

Interviewer: How would you approach this scenario?

Answer: *On arrival to this patient I would perform a full ABCDE assessment. Having established this was stable I would commence with a more detailed history. I would try to establish just how many of each medication he took. I would need to establish exactly when he took the overdose. If he were able to discuss it, I would need to discuss the circumstances that led him to taking the overdose and how he feels now that he is in the hospital. I would also want to establish risk of further attempts, including if he wrote a note, if he made efforts not to be found, and if he drank alcohol with the attempt. I would perform a full examination of the patient, including cardiovascular and neurological.*

I would request a full set of observations, an ECG, gain IV access, and would send blood tests for analysis including FBC, U&Es, LFTs, CRP, clotting, paracetamol levels, aspirin levels and iron levels. I would also consult with Toxbase to find out what the protocol is for management of the different overdoses that the patient has consumed: I would want to confirm with Toxbase but I understand that there is risk of cardiac events and the development of serotonin syndrome with sertraline overdoses, risk of gastrointestinal effects and liver failure with iron overdoses, and risk of tinnitus, drowsiness and coma with aspirin overdoses.

Interviewer: Here are some of the investigation results: what is your interpretation of them?

RESULTS:

Hb – 145 g/L   (130 – 180 g/L)
WCC – 10 x10⁹/L   (4 – 11 x10⁹/L)
Plt – 294 x10⁹/L   (150 – 450 x10⁹/L)

Na – 135 mmol/L   (133 – 146 mmol/L)
K – 4.9 mmol/L   (3.5 – 5.3 mmol/L)
Ur – 4.1 mmol/L   (2.5 – 7.8 mmol/L)
Cr – 76 mmol/L   (59 – 104 mmol/L)

ALT – 32 iU/L   (<33 iU/L)
ALP – 87 iU/L   (30 – 130 iU/L)

CRP – 6 mg/L   (<5 mg/L)

INR – 1.1

Paracetamol level – <5 mg/L
Aspirin level – 34 mg/dL
Iron Level – 200 mcg/dL

Answer: *The blood results suggest confirm that the patient has indeed had an overdose of aspirin and iron. The paracetamol levels, however, are normal, and the FBC, U&Es and LFTs are unremarkable. I do not think the CRP is significantly raised, but this would be important to keep an eye on with repeat blood tests.*

Interviewer: What would your next course of action be?

Answer: *I would ensure that the patient has aggressive fluid resuscitation running. I would arrange for their admission to a bed with a cardiac monitor. Because I am somewhat unsure of the levels of iron following an overdose, and because this overdose has involved multiple medications including sertraline, I would contact toxbase to confirm my management plan with them and see if they had any specific further advice. I would arrange for repeat blood tests in a few hours to ensure that the iron levels are falling, and would also request a further ECG to ensure the QTc remains stable.*

In addition, I would ensure that the mental health liaison team were contacted to review the patient prior to discharge, and I would ensure that I discussed the case with my senior if I had concerns about this.

Analysis: The candidate has a safe approach to this patient. They perform an initial assessment to ensure the patient isn't acutely unwell, and then begin further assessment and investigation. They also show that they know what to do in these circumstance and work within their professional limits: both by stating that they would discuss with a senior but importantly also by saying that they would look the case up on Toxbase.

Top Tip! Toxbase: this is an incredibly useful resource when dealing with complex overdoses. The website provides the common symptoms and effects of overdosing on a wide variety of medications. In complex cases, it is possible to contact pharmacologists through Toxbase's telephone service and consult with someone who has experience with managing the particular overdose. Each Trust has its unique logon details, and this is something you should ensure you are familiar with in new hospital that you work in!

Scenario 3:

A 21 year old female patient is admitted to A&E having been found confused at home by her flatmate. She is pyrexial on admission, and her admission observations are as follows: HR 89, BP 88/54, Sats 97%, RR 16, Temp 39. During her stay in A&E her GCS begins to drop and she becomes increasingly drowsy. You are the IM Stage 1 doctor and are asked to see this patient.

Interviewer: How would you approach this scenario?

Answer: *On arrival to this patient I would ensure that I perform a full A to E assessment. I am quite concerned about her airway due to her low GCS, and am also concerned about her haemodynamic status along with pyrexia.*

Therefore, my initial course of action would be to ensure that her airway was stable and protected, and that we had two large bore cannulas for IV access. I would ensure that FBC, U&Es, CRP, clotting and group and save blood tests were sent. I would also ensure blood cultures were sent at this stage. I would also ensure that I got a 500ml fluid challenge running to observe if her blood pressure responds to this.

Following these interventions, I would let my seniors know about this patient and would commence more of a thorough history (collateral, if available), and would perform a full examination. In particular, I would want to ensure there is no focal neurology and would want to perform fundoscopy.

Interviewer: Here are some of the investigation results: what is your interpretation of them?

RESULTS:

Hb – 120 g/L	(115 – 165 g/L)
WCC – 22 x10⁹/L	(4 – 11 x10⁹/L)
Plt – 256 x10⁹/L	(150 – 450 x10⁹/L)
Na – 139 mmol/L	(133 – 146 mmol/L)
K – 3.8 mmol/L	(3.5 – 5.3 mmol/L)
Ur – 3.2 mmol/L	(2.5 – 7.8 mmol/L)
Cr – 69 mmol/L	(59 – 104 mmol/L)
CRP – 189 mg/L	(<5 mg/L)
INR – 1.0	

Answer: *The blood results suggest an infective picture in this case. The haemoglobin is normal but the white cell count is significantly raised. In addition, the CRP is significantly elevated, again suggesting a picture of an active immune response. The U&Es and clotting are normal, and therefore the bloods taken together with the presentation with acute deterioration and pyrexia are consistent with an acute infection. Given the history, I am concerned about the possibility of meningitis. I would want an LP as a matter of urgency, and if this was unavailable I would treat empirically.*

Interviewer: Here are the CSF Analysis results. How would you interpret them?

CSF Analysis RESULTS:

Red Blood Cells – 8 /mm³	(0 – 10 /mm³)
WCC – 124 /mm³	(0 – 5 /mm³)
Neutrophil % – 82%	
Lymphocyte % – 18%	
Protein – 0.54 g/L	(0.15 – 0.45 g/L)
Glucose – 2.4 mmol/L	(2.8 – 4.2 mmol/L)
Opening Pressure – 25 cm H₂0	(10 – 20 cm H₂0)

Answer: Immediately, these results suggest to me that the patient is suffering with bacterial meningitis. The white blood cells are raised with a neutrophilia, the protein is raised and the glucose is low. In addition, the opening pressure is raised. All of these findings suggest to me that the patient has bacterial meningitis.

Interviewer: What would your next course of action be?

Answer: *Given the blood and CSF results along with the pyrexia, the likely diagnosis is bacterial meningitis. Therefore I would prescribe empirical antibiotics therapy (ceftriaxone). I would also ensure good supportive management was in place such as sufficient intravenous fluid rehydration.*

If the patient was not improving or responding to fluid challenges then I would further escalate this by contacting the intensive care team.

Analysis: The candidate once performs the correct initial assessment of the patient and instigates appropriate initial therapy with empirical antibiotics and fluid challenges. The investigations they request are appropriate (with the cultures being especially important in potentially infective presentations), and they identify the potential need for a lumbar puncture in this case. They also explain that they would not delay in escalating this case to their seniors.

Top Tip! You may be expected to talk the examiners through a set of CSF fluid analysis results. Take the following as an example:

WCC: Elevated, 75% lymphocytes   **Protein:** Low   **Glucose (CSF:Serum ratio):** Normal

What do you think the likely diagnosis is in this case?

The high lymphocyte count along with low protein indicate that a bacterial meningitis is not likely. This picture could represent viral meningitis, or may represent tuberculous meningitis: an important diagnosis not to forget. Make sure you are familiar with other presentations of CSF fluid (tuberculosis, bacterial, viral infections etc) prior to the interview so that you can talk the examiners through the CSF analysis with confidence.

Scenario 4:

A 47 year old patient presents to A&E vomiting copious amounts of fresh red blood. His observations on arrival are: HR 99, BP 90/60, Sats 98%, RR 16, and his Hb was 53 on arrival to A&E. You, as the IM Stage 1 doctor on the admissions team, have been asked to see him urgently as the A&E team are very concerned about him.

Interviewer: How would you approach this scenario?

Answer: *This patient's condition sounds very concerning, and so I would prioritise seeing this patient as soon as possible. On arrival, should it be obvious that he was continuing to vomit blood, I would initiate the major haemorrhage protocol and perform a full ABCDE assessment of the patient. I would want to ensure that the patient was maintaining his airway, as well as confirming that there were no other sources of bleeding.*

As long as the patient's airway was secure, I would immediately commence blood transfusions plus giving boluses of intravenous fluids due to his haemodynamic status in an attempt to resuscitate him. I would ensure that two independent Group and Save blood samples were sent for further cross-match testing in case more blood is needed after the initial protocol. During this time I would ensure a full set of bloods had been sent: a repeat FBC, U&Es, LFTs and a clotting screen.

I would also call my senior and request that they review the patient early, as well as contact the gastroenterology team and the intensive care team due to the severity of his condition.

Whilst waiting for my seniors to arrive, and once the blood was up and running, I would begin asking questions about the patient's medical background. I would attempt to ascertain a cause for the bleeding: for example, if he was known to suffer from cirrhosis then this may be a variceal bleed.

Interviewer: Here are some of the investigation results: what is your interpretation of them?

RESULTS:

Hb – 65 g/L	*(130 – 180 g/L)*
WCC – 5.3 x10⁹/L	*(4 – 11 x10⁹/L)*
Plt – 165 x10⁹/L	*(150 – 450 x10⁹/L)*
Na – 143 mmol/L	*(133 – 146 mmol/L)*
K – 4.5 mmol/L	*(3.5 – 5.3 mmol/L)*
Ur – 12.3 mmol/L	*(2.5 – 7.8 mmol/L)*
Cr – 69 mmol/L	*(59 – 104 mmol/L)*
ALT – 54 iU/L	*(<33 iU/L)*
ALP – 78 iU/L	*(30 – 130 iU/L)*
INR – 2.8	

Answer: *There are several things that are concerning in this picture. The first is the low haemoglobin. This does suggest that the bleeding is significant, and re-confirms the requirement for urgent blood transfusions. I am concerned that the urea is raised: this suggests that the patient has swallowed a significant amount of blood and therefore this bleed likely represents an upper GI bleed. The raised INR suggests that the patient has a coagulopathy, and putting this all together, along with the slightly raised ALT, my initial concerns is that the patient has an element of chronic liver disease.*

Interviewer: What would your next course of action be?

Answer: *I would continue with the blood transfusions. I would also prescribe 10mg IV Vitamin K in an attempt to resolve the coagulopathy. Should the patient continue to vomit, terlipressin may be indicated, although I would confirm this with the gastroenterology team. In addition, it appears that urgent endoscopy will be required, and this would be another reason that I would be contacting the gastroenterology team as a matter of urgency.*

Analysis: The candidate swiftly realised the urgency of the situation, and they communicated this to the interviewers well. They indicated they would perform a full A to E assessment in this patient, but importantly acknowledged that they may initiate the Major Haemorrhage Protocol (MHP) before this full assessment. Candidates shouldn't be afraid to do this: if it is obvious that the patient is haemodynamically compromised (as in this scenario) and actively vomiting blood, then the ABCDE assessment from the end of the bed is obvious enough, and the MHP can and should be triggered early.

Other important and successful points in this scenario are the early involvement of seniors and of the other important clinical teams: gastroenterology and intensive care medicine. They talked about the important investigations to perform: the full set of bloods along with the endoscopy. The candidate also found the clues in the bloods appropriately – the haemoglobin is obvious enough, but it was important to pick up on the raised urea and clotting abnormality.

> ***Top Tip!*** The Major Haemorrhage Protocol is a rapid way of obtaining blood products in an emergency. Though there may be variations in individual Trusts, the main products included are:
> - 4 Units of RBCs (Universal Donor: O negative)
> - 4 Units of Fresh Frozen Plasma

Scenario 5:

A 57 year old man is admitted with what he describes as the worst headache he has ever experienced. His observations on arrival are: HR 64, BP 130/92, Sats 98%, RR 16, Temp 36.9. During assessment in the A&E department his GCS begins to drop. You are the IM Stage 1 doctor and are asked to clerk this patient.

Interviewer: How would you approach this scenario?

Answer: *I am concerned in this patient about the possibility of a subarachnoid haemorrhage. I would perform a full A to E assessment on arrival to this patient. Following this, I would perform a full history and examination, paying close attention to the Neurological examination to identify any clinical signs. It sounds as if the patient's GCS is starting to drop, and so this is very concerning. I would ensure that he has a stable airway, using adjuncts as necessary, and then would contact my senior urgently to inform them of the situation. I would also discuss the patient early with the neurology and neurosurgery team, as well as potentially the anaesthetists and intensive care team if I was concerned about preserving the patient's airway.*

The patient would also require additional investigation. They would need to have an ECG, a full set of blood tests (including FBC, U&Es, LFTs, CRP and clotting screen), and would also need urgent CT head imaging to be done. Depending on the results of this and the clinical suspicion of a bleed, the patient may also require lumbar puncture (sending for xanthochromia) to further investigate the possibility of a SAH.

Interviewer: Here are some of the investigation results: what is your interpretation of them?

RESULTS:

Hb – 150 g/L	(130 – 180 g/L)
WCC – 6.7 x10⁹/L	(4 – 11 x10⁹/L)
Plt – 167 x10⁹/L	(150 – 450 x10⁹/L)
Na – 141 mmol/L	(133 – 146 mmol/L)
K – 3.5 mmol/L	(3.5 – 5.3 mmol/L)
Ur – 6.7 mmol/L	(2.5 – 7.8 mmol/L)
Cr – 74 mmol/L	(59 – 104 mmol/L)
CRP – <5 mg/L	(<5 mg/L)
ALT – 20 iU/L	(<33 iU/L)
ALP – 45 iU/L	(30 – 130 iU/L)
INR – 1.0	

Answer: *The blood tests show normal values: this means that my suspicion of a possible sub-arachnoid haemorrhage is still quite high. The normal WCC and CRP go some way to making an infective cause of his headache (though unlikely from the history) even less likely.*

Interviewer: What would your next course of action be?

Answer: *As I mentioned earlier, I think the important next steps would be CT imaging of the patient's brain, followed by lumbar puncture looking for xanthochromia.*

I would also monitor the patient's observations for any changes: I know there is a significant risk of further bleeding if the blood pressure is too high and so I would titrate the blood pressure to keep it below 140 mmHg. I would also treat the patient's pain with analgesia, if the pain was ongoing, and would monitor for seizure activity and treat as appropriate.

Analysis: The candidate correctly identifies the most serious differential diagnosis that they must rule out, and they perform the initial assessment safely. They identify that the GCS is reported to be dropping, and so realise that airway protection is going to be vital in this case. The candidate also states that they will escalate this to seniors early, as the patient has the potential to rapidly decompensate if their GCS continues to drop. The candidate shows they know the appropriate investigation (CT and LP) in these cases, but also note that it will depend on the specific clinical scenario whether and when the LP must be performed.

Top Tip! Be prepared to talk through the Glasgow Coma Scale (GCS) during the interview. This is a clinical scale developed to assess patients' level of consciousness, and so stratify seriousness of head injury. There are three components:

Eyes:	Verbal:	Motor:
4. Open	5. Conversing normally	6. Obeys commands
3. Open to voice	4. Conversing but disoriented	5. Localizes to pain
2. Open to pain	3. Inappropriate words	4. Withdraws from pain
1. Not opening	2. Incomprehensible noises	3. Abnormal flexion
	1. No sounds	2. Abnormal extension
		1. No motor response

Adding the best responses in each category gives a score from 3-15, with lower scores indicating a reduced level of consciousness

---

Scenario 6:

A 38 year old female patient presents to the A&E department with acute abdominal pain radiating to her back and vomiting. Her HR is 94, BP 103/68, Sats 96%, RR 17 and Temp 37.3. You, as the clerking IM Stage 1 doctor, have been asked to see her.

Interviewer: How would you approach this scenario?

Answer: *I would perform a full ABCDE assessment on my arrival to this patient. Judging by the observations, one of my concerns is with the slightly low blood pressure, and with the clinical picture potentially suggestive of pancreatitis, aggressive fluid resuscitation may be important in this patient. I would prescribe a fluid bolus initially in an attempt to correct the hypotension.*

Once I was happy with the full A through E assessment I would take a full history from the patient, finding more out about the pain and vomiting. I would want to know about the patient's past medical history (including whether she has a history of gallstones), and would want to ask her questions about her alcohol consumption.

For investigations, I would want an ECG and a pregnancy test. In addition, I would request a full set of blood tests. I would request FBC, U&Es, LFTs, CRP, clotting screen, and Amylase and Lipase (if available). I would then consider requesting an abdominal ultrasound scan.

Interviewer: Here are some of the investigation results: what is your interpretation of them?

RESULTS:

Hb – 124 g/L	*(115 – 165 g/L)*
WCC – 12 x10⁹/L	*(4 – 11 x10⁹/L)*
Plt – 234 x10⁹/L	*(150 – 450 x10⁹/L)*
Na – 134 mmol/L	*(133 – 146 mmol/L)*
K – 4.2 mmol/L	*(3.5 – 5.3 mmol/L)*
Ur – 4.5 mmol/L	*(2.5 – 7.8 mmol/L)*
Cr – 81 mmol/L	*(59 – 104 mmol/L)*
ALT – 23 iU/L	*(<33 iU/L)*
ALP – 34 iU/L	*(30 – 130 iU/L)*
CRP – 68 mg/L	*(<5 mg/L)*
Amylase – 234 iU/dL	*(28 –100 iU/dL)*

Pregnancy Test - Negative

Answer: *The patient's U&Es and LFTs are normal. The white blood cells and CRP are raised indicating an inflammatory picture. The amylase is significantly raised, which means my initial diagnosis of pancreatitis is now extremely likely.*

Interviewer: What would your next course of action be?

Answer: *I would commence treatment with the fluid resuscitation that I mentioned earlier. I would prescribe analgesia for the patient's pain. I would provide supplemental oxygen to ensure adequate tissue oxygenation. I would also arrange an abdominal ultrasound scan.*

I would discuss the case with my senior – and if there were any signs of the patient becoming more unwell then I would have a low threshold for discussion with the intensive care team. If the patient has a strong history of gallstones or this is confirmed on imaging, then the patient may require ERCP.

Analysis: The candidate carries out a thorough initial assessment, and investigates and manages the patient appropriately. They correctly identify their main differential diagnosis. They involve their seniors at an appropriate stage, and confirm that if there is any sign of the patient deteriorating further then the patient will need to be reviewed by, and likely managed in, intensive care.

Top Tip! Risk stratification/prediction of severity can come up when discussing pancreatitis. The common scores used are the APACHE II score and the Glasgow criteria. We would recommend familiarity with at least the Glasgow criteria. They are:

- P – PaO2 < 8kPa
- A – Age > 55 years
- N – Neutrophilia (WCC > 15×10^9/L)
- C – Calcium < 2mmol/L
- R – Renal (Urea > 16mmol/L)
- E – Enzymes (LDH > 600IU/L, AST > 200IU/L)
- A – Albumin <32g/L
- S – Sugar (blood glucose > 10mmol/L)

A score of 3 or more indicates the patient has presented with a severe episode of pancreatitis and may warrant urgent transfer to the intensive care unit.

Scenario 7:

An 18 year old female patient is admitted with acute shortness of breath. She has a background of asthma, and is noted to be struggling to complete full sentences. Her observations on arrival are: HR 80, BP 110/72, Sats 91%, RR 28, Temp 37.4. Her peak flow is 35% of her best. You are the IM1 doctor on call, and have been asked to see this patient in A&E.

Interviewer: How would you approach this scenario?

Answer: *I am worried about an acute severe exacerbation of asthma in this patient. This is suggested by the low peak flow and her inability to complete full sentences. I would immediately perform a full ABCDE assessment on the patient. I would particularly look for breathing signs during this assessment, including wheeze and a silent chest, being particularly concerned if I thought the latter were present. I would also ensure that her peak flows are re-measured at regular intervals, as if they drop under 33%, or if the patient tires further, then this would fall into the classification of life-threatening asthma attack.*

It is clear that this patient needs urgent treatment, and so I would commence back-to-back 5mg salbutamol nebulisers on oxygen, as well as commencing ipratropium nebulisers. I would follow the British Thoracic Society guidelines when escalating therapy in this patient, and I would involve my seniors early when making management decisions about escalating her therapy. Escalated options include intravenous steroid therapy, and consideration of magnesium sulphate injections.

The patient also requires investigating further, including blood tests such as an FBC and U&Es, and repeat peak flow measurements. I would also perform an Arterial Blood Gas in this patient due to her low oxygen saturation. If the patient were stable enough then I would also want a Chest X-Ray.

Interviewer: Here are some of the investigation results: what is your interpretation of them?

RESULTS:

Hb – 116 g/L	*(115 – 165 g/L)*
WCC – 11.2 x10⁹/L	*(4 – 11 x10⁹/L)*
Plt – 329 x10⁹/L	*(150 – 450 x10⁹/L)*
Na – 138 mmol/L	*(133 – 146 mmol/L)*
K – 4.9 mmol/L	*(3.5 – 5.3 mmol/L)*
Ur – 2.9 mmol/L	*(2.5 – 7.8 mmol/L)*
Cr – 63 mmol/L	*(59 – 104 mmol/L)*
CRP – 15 mg/L	*(<5 mg/L)*

Repeat PEFR – 34% of best

pH – 7.36	*(7.35 – 7.45)*
PaCO2 – 5.8 kPa	*(4.7 – 6.0 kPa)*
PaO2 – 9 kPa	*(11 – 13 kPa)*
HCO3 – 23 mEg/L	*(22 – 26 mEg/L)*

Answer: *The white blood cells are slightly raised and the CRP only slightly up, and so I think this is likely a picture of the inflammatory state rather than an acute infection: though the asthma exacerbation could be triggered by a viral infection. The U&Es are normal and the patient is not anaemic.*

The repeat PEFR is consistent with the first measurement, but there is the possibility of a slight trend down and so I would want to make sure this is repeated.

The arterial blood gas shows that the patient is hypoxic – this is a concern and is why I have given the patient oxygen. However, the pH and PaCO2 are normal which is more reassuring, but this gas warrants repeating following several rounds of treatment to ensure that the PaCO2 is not rising (and that the PaO2 is responding).

Interviewer: What would your next course of action be?

Answer: *I would continue with the back-to-back nebulisers, and continue down the BTS treatment pathway of an acute severe asthma attack. However, given all of the above, I am concerned about this patient's risk for further deterioration, and so would contact the intensive care team to make them aware of the patient at this early stage as it is clear that there is a significant potential for deterioration.*

Analysis: The candidate has talked through this scenario in an organised and professional manner. They are aware of the urgency of the situation, and have involved their seniors early as well as commencing immediate treatment with oxygen and nebulisers. They have identified the seriousness of the attack, and mentioned to the interviewers that they know where to look for further information (the British Thoracic Society guidelines). They also discuss appropriate investigation and further escalation as required.

Top Tip! British Thoracic Society Guidelines make for essential reading when revising the treatment of asthma. These can be found at: https://www.brit-thoracic.org.uk

When revising these guidelines, ensure that you can identify the seriousness of the asthma attack based on the clinical criteria outlined in their guidelines. This is essential because it guides the treatment that you give, and determines when escalation to intensive care should be performed.

Scenario 8:

A 68 year old female patient with a background of COPD presents to A&E with increasing wheeze over the last few weeks, and with a slightly purulent cough that she hasn't been able to shake. Her observations on arrival are: HR 80, BP 137/93, Sats 89%, RR 26, Temp 37.9. You are the IM Stage 1 doctor and have been asked to clerk this patient.

Interviewer: How would you approach this scenario?

Answer: *My first course of action would be to perform a full A through E assessment of this patient, ensuring that her airway, breathing and circulation were intact. It sounds like this patient is wheezy and tachypnoeic, and so before further history and examination I would probably perform an ABG and commence salbutamol nebulisers in an attempt to improve her respiratory rate and determine how badly her acid-base balance has been affected.*

I would then take a full history and examine this patient with particular focus on the respiratory system. Amongst other items, I would want to determine if there is a formal diagnosis of COPD, and how many infections she has had over the last year. I would want to isolate if there were any obvious signs of consolidation or wheeze on exam. I would aim to maintain her oxygen saturations within the 88-92% range at this time unless I was concerned that she was becoming acutely hypoxic in which case I would escalate the oxygen therapy as required.

I would investigate with bloods (FBC, U&Es, LFTs, CRP, and clotting) and an arterial blood gas. I would monitor the temperature closely as there appears to be a low-grade pyrexia, but this wouldn't trigger criteria for blood cultures at this stage. I would however arrange for sputum culture to be sent and would also request that the patient's urinary legionella and pneumocystis antigens be tested. I would obtain a chest x-ray, looking for any obvious consolidation, and perhaps signs of chronic COPD changes (including hyperexpanded fields).

Interviewer: Here are some of the investigation results: what is your interpretation of them?

RESULTS:

Hb – 160 g/L	(115 – 165 g/L)
WCC – 14.3 x10^9/L	(4 – 11 x10^9/L)
Plt – 343 x10^9/L	(150 – 450 x10^9/L)
Na – 144 mmol/L	(133 – 146 mmol/L)
K – 5.0 mmol/L	(3.5 – 5.3 mmol/L)
Ur – 7.3 mmol/L	(2.5 – 7.8 mmol/L)
Cr – 110 mmol/L	(59 – 104 mmol/L)
ALT – 30 iU/L	(<33 iU/L)
ALP – 87 iU/L	(30 – 130 iU/L)
CRP – 98 mg/L	(<5 mg/L)
INR – 0.9	
pH – 7.32	(7.35 – 7.45)
PaCO2 – 6.6 kPa	(4.7 – 6.0 kPa)
PaO2 – 9.3 kPa	(11 – 13 kPa)
HCO3 – 27.3 mEg/L	(22 – 26 mEg/L)

Answer: *The white blood cells and CRP are raised: this makes me think there may be an underlying infection triggering this exacerbation of COPD.*

The U&Es suggest that the patient may be a little dry, and so I would commence fluid rehydration therapy.

I am somewhat concerned about the ABG: the patient demonstrates a partially compensated respiratory acidosis. I am concerned about the high PaCO2 as the patient may be entering type 2 respiratory failure.

Interviewer: What would your next course of action be?

Answer: *I would continue with salbutamol nebulisers, add ipratropium nebulisers and would start the patient on a course of 30mg prednisolone orally for 5 days.*

I feel that the patient likely has an infective cause to this presentation – given the cough, possible low-grade pyrexia, and investigation results – and so, in addition, I would start on appropriate antibiotic therapy. At this stage this sounds like an infective exacerbation of COPD and so I would commence doxycycline, however if the chest x ray revealed an underlying pneumonia then I would treat with the appropriate antibiotic relative to her underlying CURB65 score.

I would want to try the patient with the initial therapy I mentioned, but if the PaCO2 does not improve on repeat ABG testing then this is an indication that the patient may require non-invasive ventilation, and so I would escalate the patient to my seniors, enquiring as to the possibility of a non-invasive ventilation bed either on a respiratory ward or medical high-dependency.

I would also ensure that I made a referral to the community outreach COPD team in hospital in an attempt to ensure the patient would be discharged in a timely fashion, should she improve with the above treatment.

Analysis: This is a thorough run-through of dealing with a patient presenting with what is likely an exacerbation of COPD. The candidate appropriately assessed the patient acutely, and commenced the correct treatment in this case. They demonstrated good investigative knowledge – not forgetting to request a sputum culture and urinary antigen testing. They also mentioned that they would refer to the community COPD team in hospital to try and facilitate patient discharge, an important thing to remember when part of the admitting team.

> ***Top Tip!*** Ensure you are familiar with the different findings that can be present on an ABG as they are a common source of data interpretation in the interview.

Scenario 9:

An 82 year old male nursing home resident is brought to A&E as the nursing home staff noticed that he started coughing quite severely since lunch. His observations on arrival are: HR 64, BP 130/92, Sats 92%, RR 24, Temp 36.9. You are the clerking IM Stage 1 doctor and have been asked to see this patient.

Interviewer: How would you approach this scenario?

Answer: *My immediate thought is that this patient may be suffering from an aspiration pneumonitis/pneumonia. This is due to his background of living in a nursing home and the fact that he started coughing following a meal. On arrival to the patient I would perform a full A through E assessment. The observations suggest to me that he may be a little hypoxic, and so I would commence oxygen therapy.*

Once satisfied with the rest of the A to E assessment, I would then turn to performing a full history and thorough clinical examination. I would want to determine what exactly happened and if the patient can remember the events. I would want to know if he has known problems with his swallow, and this may require collateral history from the nursing home. If I felt he was likely to have an unsafe swallow (I could ask him to take a small sip of water to give me an idea) then I would make him nil by mouth and commence him on IV fluid supplementation.

I would determine whether there were any obvious signs on clinical examination of pneumonia or respiratory pathology. I would ensure bloods are sent (including FBC, U&Es, LFTs, and CRP). I would try to send a sample of his sputum for culture and perform urinary antigen testing. I would request an urgent chest x ray, as if the patient has aspirated then he may show signs of this in his right lower lobe.

Interviewer: Here are some of the investigation results: what is your interpretation of them?

RESULTS:

Hb – 125 g/L	*(130 – 180 g/L)*
WCC – 10.3 x10⁹/L	*(4 – 11 x10⁹/L)*
Plt – 159 x10⁹/L	*(150 – 450 x10⁹/L)*
Na – 139 mmol/L	*(133 – 146 mmol/L)*
K – 3.9 mmol/L	*(3.5 – 5.3 mmol/L)*
Ur – 7.1 mmol/L	*(2.5 – 7.8 mmol/L)*
Cr – 96 mmol/L	*(59 – 104 mmol/L)*
ALT – 27 iU/L	*(<33 iU/L)*
ALP – 54 iU/L	*(30 – 130 iU/L)*
CRP – 7 mg/L	*(<5 mg/L)*

Answer: *The patient is slightly anaemic, and so sending haematinics would be appropriate. His U&Es are within normal limits, though the urea is at the upper limit of normal, as is the creatinine, and so I would look to see if we had a baseline on the system and if not I would start slow IV fluid rehydration to try to reduce the risk of the patient developing an AKI. The patient's inflammatory markers are essentially within normal limits, and this would fit with an acute presentation of a possible aspiration pneumonitis.*

Interviewer: What would your next course of action be?

Answer: *I would continue with supportive management, and would await the chest x ray. If the patient was not improving within 24-48 hours then I would consider further management with empirical antibiotics such as levofloxacin, and potential further investigations such as CT imaging or bronchoalveolar lavage after discussion with a senior.*

Analysis: The candidate correctly makes the initial diagnosis but does so in a way that shows that they realise the initial presentation in cases such as this is with aspiration pneumonitis as opposed to aspiration pneumonia – which potentially can develop later. Therefore, they correctly assess and treat the patient in the acute situation, and they also avoid inappropriate antibiotic therapy. They clarify this, however, with knowledge of what they would do should the patient not be improving.

Top Tip! Aspiration pneumonitis is a common presentation from nursing homes. The aspirate is often aspirated down the right main bronchus (due to it being a more "vertical" route into the lungs), and so that is frequently where chest x ray changes are seen. It is also important to remember that these patients usually don't require antibiotic therapy initially – at this acute stage there is likely no infection present, and so simply providing supportive care as required is the treatment. If the patient starts to deteriorate (usually 24-48 hours later), then this is when you should consider repeat investigation and possible antibiotic therapy. Local policy documents differ on when and what antibiotic to prescribe, and so it is always important to check there first.

Scenario 10:

A 53 year old male patient has been admitted with a pneumonia and is on the respiratory ward. He reports to the nursing staff that he has developed severe crushing central chest pain. His HR is 74, his BP is 153/90, Sats 97%, RR 18 and Temp 37. You are the IM Stage 1 doctor on call and have been asked to assess this patient.

Interviewer: How would you approach this scenario?

Answer: *The first thing I would do on arrival to this patient is to perform a full ABCDE assessment and ensure that he is clinically stable. If he was still in chest pain I would ensure that an ECG is performed urgently, as well as providing initial treatment for ACS as my suspicions are high: I would provide oxygen, morphine, 300mg Aspirin and a GTN spray.*

If there were ST elevation changes on the ECG then I would contact my local PCI centre urgently, and see whether I could arrange transfer for treatment.

Following this, I would continue my full history and examination: I would want to ensure I identified exactly when the pain began, the character of the pain, if he has had it before, if he has any cardiac history, as well as completing my full systems review and background social and family history. I would perform a full cardiology examination, looking for any heart murmurs or signs of cardiac decompensation.

I would then begin investigating the cause for the patient's presentation. I mentioned the ECG earlier, and would have this repeated urgently if there were any further episodes of chest pain. It would be important to perform an initial set of bloods, including FBC, U&Es, clotting and also a troponin. I would then need to correlate this result with a 6-hour troponin to observe if there were any dynamic changes. I would also perform a chest x-ray.

Interviewer: Here are some of the investigation results: what is your interpretation of them?

RESULTS:

Hb – 143 g/L   *(130 – 180 g/L)*
WCC – 10.9 x10⁹/L   *(4 – 11 x10⁹/L)*
Plt – 402 x10⁹/L   *(150 – 450 x10⁹/L)*

Na – 142 mmol/L   *(133 – 146 mmol/L)*
K – 4.9 mmol/L   *(3.5 – 5.3 mmol/L)*
Ur – 4.8 mmol/L   *(2.5 – 7.8 mmol/L)*
Cr – 73 mmol/L   *(59 – 104 mmol/L)*

INR 1.0

Troponin T – 25 ng/L   *(<14 ng/L)*

Repeat Troponin T – 281 ng/L   *(<14 ng/L)*

Answer: *The FBC and U&Es are normal with the exception of the slightly raised white blood cells: though this could be explained by the fact that the patient was admitted with pneumonia. The patient's troponin has shown a significant rise at the second measurement, and this confirms the fact that he has indeed had an acute coronary episode.*

Interviewer: What would your next course of action be?

Answer: *Given the fact that I have confirmed ACS in this patient I would prescribe fondaparinux. If the ECG showed ST elevation then I would call my local PCI centre to try to arrange transfer, and if the ECG did not show signs of ST elevation I would arrange for transfer to a Coronary Care Unit.*

The patient should also have secondary prevention medication prescribed: these would include dual antiplatelet therapy, a statin, a beta-blocker and an angiotensin converting enzyme inhibitor (ACEi).

I would also inform my senior about this case to make sure they were happy with the management plan that I have initiated, and to let them know if they were moving to the Coronary Care Unit.

Analysis: Once again, the candidate performs a successful initial assessment of the patient. They manage the patient appropriately, and identify that the patient may need transfer for PCI therapy if certain criteria are met. They correctly investigate the cause for the patient's presentation, and take an appropriate history and examination.

The interviewers may, in this case, give the interviewee a piece of paper with information regarding the patient's blood test results (including troponin) and ask them to make a decision regarding whether the patient requires admission or not. Finally, the patient correctly identifies the required secondary prevention.

> ***Top Tip!*** Acute Coronary Syndrome is a common interview topic, and the treatment for this should flow off the tip of your tongue. Be sure to revise ECGs, as the interviewers may show you an ECG with an infarct present, and may ask you to identify the abnormality, including where it is anatomically located.

Scenario 11:

You are the IM Stage 1 doctor looking after the wards in a District General Hospital. A 37 year old male patient was admitted two days ago following his first ever seizure with no apparent cause found, and is being prepared for discharge. However, the nurse calls you overnight informing you that the patient has become quite confused, aggressive, and is seeing objects that aren't there. She says he looks hot and sweaty, but doesn't have recent observations.

Interviewer: How would you approach this scenario?

Answer: *I am concerned in this case that the patient may be withdrawing from alcohol, and possible may have developed Delirium Tremens. This is an emergency and so I would attend the patient as soon as possible. Indeed, the withdrawal may have been the initial reason for his presentation with a seizure. I would ask the nurse on the phone that, if she felt the situation was safe enough, she should perform a full set of observations and I would be there as soon as possible.*

On arrival I would perform a full A through E assessment of the patient. I would then try to engage with him in conversation and determine how unwell he actually was at this moment in time. I would look through the observations and commence further investigation, whilst trying to obtain a quick alcohol consumption history from the patient if he were able to provide this.

I would investigate the patient by performing an ECG and a capillary blood glucose reading. I would send a full set of bloods, including FBC, U&Es, LFTs, CRP, Bone Profile, magnesium, glucose, amylase and a clotting screen. I would perform an arterial blood gas looking for signs of metabolic acidosis. I would review the requirement for CT imaging of the patient's head depending on if any imaging has been performed since arrival and if the patient has had any trauma to his head since being in hospital.

Interviewer: Here are some of the investigation results: what is your interpretation of them?

RESULTS:

Hb – 137 g/L	(130 – 180 g/L)
WCC – 5.2 x10^9/L	(4 – 11 x10^9/L)
Plt – 158 x10^9/L	(150 – 450 x10^9/L)
Na – 135 mmol/L	(133 – 146 mmol/L)
K – 3.6 mmol/L	(3.5 – 5.3 mmol/L)
Ur – 2.6 mmol/L	(2.5 – 7.8 mmol/L)
Cr – 73 mmol/L	(59 – 104 mmol/L)
Corrected Ca – 2.3 mmol/L	(2.2 – 2.6 mmol/L)
PO4 – 0.9 mmol/L	(0.8 – 1.4 mmol/L)
Magnesium – 0.8 mmol/L	(0.7 – 1.0 mmol/L)
ALT – 46 iU/L	(<33 iU/L)
ALP – 65 iU/L	(30 – 130 iU/L)
CRP – <5 mg/L	(<5 mg/L)
Amylase – 43 iU/dL	(28 –100 iU/dL)
Serum Glucose – 7 mmol/L	(<7.8 mmol/L
INR – 1.1	

Answer: *Most of the blood tests given here are normal. The patient's ALT is slightly raised, which could fit with a picture of liver-disease. However, and reassuringly from a possible seizure point of view, the Magnesium, Calcium, Phosphate and glucose are normal, along with the other electrolytes. The bloods also serve to reduce the likelihood of other potential causes of delirium such as infection and electrolyte disturbances.*

Interviewer: What would your next course of action be?

Answer: *I would commence treatment for alcohol withdrawal: I would follow my local Trust's protocol in prescribing benzodiazepines for the patient (usually chlordiazepoxide, but I may consider diazepam in this case) as well as prescribing high-dose pabrinex. I would inform my senior about the presentation of the patient, and ensure that they knew that I may need to escalate this patient further if he did not respond to the above therapy.*

Analysis: The candidate has a good patient-centred approach, and identifies that they need more information about the patient's observations but only as long as this wouldn't affect the safety of staff on the ward. They correctly identify the key to the scenario, which is that it is likely that the patient has had a diagnosis of alcohol withdrawal missed. The candidate also identifies that the patient is acutely and severely unwell, and that they need urgent medical attention. They candidate investigates the patient in an effective and thorough manner, and initiates the appropriate therapy in cases of alcohol withdrawal. They also explain that they would contact their senior, which is very appropriate in this case due to the potential severity of Delirium Tremens.

> ***Top Tip!*** Acute alcohol withdrawal and decompensated liver disease are other common cases that come up in interviews and so it is important to be familiar with the diagnosis and management of these conditions.

Scenario 12:

An 84 year old female nursing home resident with Alzheimer's disease is brought to A&E as she has been found increasingly confused at the home. She is unable to give an accurate history, but understands that she is in hospital. Her HR is 92, BP 94/60, Sats 98%, RR 18 and Temp 37.8. You are the IM Stage 1 doctor on the acute medicine team and have been asked to clerk this patient.

Interviewer: How would you approach this scenario?

Answer: *This patient sounds quite unwell and possibly delirious. I would perform a full A through E assessment on arrival to the patient. It sounds as if the patient is not able to provide a full history for me, which is a concern. I would therefore have to work on the clinical signs (and would perform a full clinical exam to look for any clues as to what might be going on – I am leaning towards infection in this case), and any collateral history that I can obtain from the nursing home team.*

I would perform a urine dip, an ECG, and a chest x-ray. If the patient was coughing I would send a sputum culture. I would ask for a full set of blood tests including FBC, U&Es, CRP and clotting. I would probably perform blood cultures in this case: the patient has a low-grade pyrexia and is acutely confused and so as such I would want to investigate for the possibility of septicaemia.

Interviewer: Here are some of the investigation results: what is your interpretation of them?

RESULTS:

Hb – 117 g/L	(115 – 165 g/L)
WCC – 11.4 x10⁹/L	(4 – 11 x10⁹/L)
Plt – 167 x10⁹/L	(150 – 450 x10⁹/L)
Na – 133 mmol/L	(133 – 146 mmol/L)
K – 4.3 mmol/L	(3.5 – 5.3 mmol/L)
Ur – 10.9 mmol/L	(2.5 – 7.8 mmol/L)
Cr – 143 mmol/L	(59 – 104 mmol/L)
CRP – 34 mg/L	(<5 mg/L)
INR – 1.0	

Answer: *The blood tests suggest to me that there is an infective picture present: with both the white blood cells and CRP being raised. However, the blood tests also suggest the presence of an acute kidney injury. Dehydration is another potential cause of delirium, and so my working diagnosis at this stage would be that the patient has both an infection of unknown origin in addition to acute kidney injury.*

Interviewer: What would your next course of action be?

Answer: *I would want to assess the patient's capacity: it sounds like this may be borderline based on the scenario description and so I would want to confirm either way. If I felt the patient did not have capacity then it would be important to complete a Deprivation of Liberty Safeguard (DOLS) form, and to ensure we are acting in the patient's best interests.*

I feel that the patient's low blood pressure and marginally elevated pulse, along with the U&E results, suggest that she may be somewhat fluid deplete, and so would commence intravenous fluid rehydration at a cautious pace given her age.

As I mentioned, I would attempt to gain a further collateral history from the nursing home. I would also try to contact the next of kin as I feel this is in the patient's best interests and would attempt to uncover more about the patient's past medical history. If this were not possible then I would discuss with my senior and suggest that I think that the patient may have an infection that we are struggling to localise (depending on results of the above investigations), and that the best course of action may be to cover the patient with broad-spectrum antibiotics whilst we completed our investigations and hope that the patient's confusion settles with appropriate therapy.

Analysis: As you have seen so far, the key thing is that the candidate works safely, always assessing the patient's condition from baseline, and works within their competence, asking for senior advice when required. In this scenario, the candidate also pays close attention to the patient's observations and identifies that they could probably use some intravenous fluids, which forms part of the candidate's management plan. They also feel that the presentation and low-grade pyrexia indicate a possible infection. Importantly, they inform the interviewers that they would act safely in this situation where they don't know the likely source as they suggest broad-spectrum antibiotics as appropriate treatment options.

Top Tip! Don't forget the utility and importance of a collateral history in cases where the patient is unconscious or otherwise unable to give an accurate history. In cases such as this one, also don't forget the importance of a capacity assessment and completion of a DOLS: the interviewers want to know that you have practical experience of seeing patients like this and know the full medical and legal implications of managing them.

Further Example Scenarios

We now cover some additional scenarios that may well come up during the interview. We do not provide full sample answers, but rather the questions as they may be asked in the interview (following the format used above), and example investigation results. The idea is that you may wish to work through these scenarios with a friend who is also preparing for the IM interviews. There is an answer page detailing the main aspects to include in each of these scenarios at the end.

Additional Scenario 1:

A 35 year old male patient presents to the A&E department with a history of weight loss, tiredness, and very severe diarrhoea for the last several days. He attends with his male partner. His HR is 87, his BP is 118/70, Sats 98%, RR 18 and Temp 37.8. You are the IM Stage 1 doctor on call and have been asked to clerk this patient.

Interviewer: How would you approach this scenario?

Interviewer: Here are some of the investigation results: what is your interpretation of them?

RESULTS:

Hb – 119 g/L	(130 – 180 g/L)
WCC – 3.4 x10⁹/L	(4 – 11 x10⁹/L)
Lymphocytes – 0.3 x10⁹/L	(1 - 3 x10⁹/L)
Neutrophils – 3.0 x10⁹/L	(2 - 7 x10⁹/L)
Plt – 172 x10⁹/L	(150 – 450 x10⁹/L)
Na – 141 mmol/L	(133 – 146 mmol/L)
K – 4.1 mmol/L	(3.5 – 5.3 mmol/L)
Ur – 8.9 mmol/L	(2.5 – 7.8 mmol/L)
Cr – 131 mmol/L	(59 – 104 mmol/L)
CRP – 84 mg/L	(<5 mg/L)

Interviewer: What would your next course of action be?

Additional Scenario 2:

You are the IM Stage 1 doctor on call. You are asked to clerk a 21 year old male patient who presents with vomiting and severe abdominal pain. His observations on arrival are: HR is 98, his BP is 112/68, Sats 97%, RR 20 and Temp 37. His partner reports that he has become increasingly drowsy since arriving in the department.

Interviewer: How would you approach this scenario?

Interviewer: Here are some of the investigation results: what is your interpretation of them?

RESULTS:

Hb – 117 g/L	*(130 – 180 g/L)*
WCC – 12.1 x10⁹/L	*(4 – 11 x10⁹/L)*
Plt – 291 x10⁹/L	*(150 – 450 x10⁹/L)*
Na – 143 mmol/L	*(133 – 146 mmol/L)*
K – 5.2 mmol/L	*(3.5 – 5.3 mmol/L)*
Ur – 6.9 mmol/L	*(2.5 – 7.8 mmol/L)*
Cr – 101 mmol/L	*(59 – 104 mmol/L)*
CRP – <5 mg/L	*(<5 mg/L)*
INR – 1.0	
Glucose – 21 mmol/L	*(<7 mmol/L)*
pH – 7.29	*(7.35 – 7.45)*
PaCO2 – 5.2 kPa	*(4.7 – 6.0 kPa)*
PaO2 – 12.3 kPa	*(11 – 13 kPa)*
HCO3 – 18 mEg/L	*(22 – 26 mEg/L)*

Urinalysis:
Protein – +
Blood – Negative
Glucose – ++
Ketones – +++

Interviewer: What would your next course of action be?

Additional Scenario 3:

A 25 year old woman presents to the MAU with nausea, vomiting and abdominal pain with occasional diarrhoea for the last three days. She denies any other symptoms of note. Her HR is 73, her BP is 120/83, Sats 97%, RR 16 and Temp 36.9. You have been asked to clerk her in.

Interviewer: How would you approach this scenario?

Interviewer: Here are some of the investigation results: what is your interpretation of them?

RESULTS:

Hb – 132 g/L	(115 – 165 g/L)
WCC – 14.9 x10^9/L	(4 – 11 x10^9/L)
Plt – 239 x10^9/L	(150 – 450 x10^9/L)
Na – 140 mmol/L	(133 – 146 mmol/L)
K – 3.9 mmol/L	(3.5 – 5.3 mmol/L)
Ur – 7.9 mmol/L	(2.5 – 7.8 mmol/L)
Cr – 92 mmol/L	(59 – 104 mmol/L)
CRP – 59 mg/L	(<5 mg/L)

Interviewer: What would your next course of action be?

Additional Scenario 4:

A 57 year old lady presents to the Medical Assessment Unit with left leg erythema and swelling. You have been asked to clerk her in and arrange for investigation as required. Her HR is 82, her BP is 133/94, Sats 97%, RR 18 and Temp 37.

Interviewer: How would you approach this scenario?

Interviewer: Here are some of the investigation results: what is your interpretation of them?

RESULTS:

Hb – 127 g/L	*(115 – 165 g/L)*
WCC – 7.4 x10⁹/L	*(4 – 11 x10⁹/L)*
Plt – 360 x10⁹/L	*(150 – 450 x10⁹/L)*
Na – 140 mmol/L	*(133 – 146 mmol/L)*
K – 4.7 mmol/L	*(3.5 – 5.3 mmol/L)*
Ur – 3.9 mmol/L	*(2.5 – 7.8 mmol/L)*
Cr – 64 mmol/L	*(59 – 104 mmol/L)*
CRP – <5 mg/L	*(<5 mg/L)*
INR – 1.1	
D-Dimer 280 ng/ml	*(<230 ng/ml)*

Interviewer: What would your next course of action be?

Additional Scenario 5:

A 34 year old intravenous drug user presents with recurrent fevers and shortness of breath. On examination it has been reported that the patient has evidence of splinter haemorrhages and a murmur. His HR is 88, his BP is 123/78, Sats 95%, RR 17 and Temp 37.9. You are the IM Stage 1 doctor on call and have been asked to assess the patient.

Interviewer: How would you approach this scenario?

Interviewer: Here are some of the investigation results: what is your interpretation of them?

RESULTS:

Hb – 123 g/L	(130 – 180 g/L)
WCC – 11.9 x10^9/L	(4 – 11 x10^9/L)
Plt – 181 x10^9/L	(150 – 450 x10^9/L)
Na – 135 mmol/L	(133 – 146 mmol/L)
K – 3.8 mmol/L	(3.5 – 5.3 mmol/L)
Ur – 5.8 mmol/L	(2.5 – 7.8 mmol/L)
Cr – 73 mmol/L	(59 – 104 mmol/L)
CRP – 124 mg/L	(<5 mg/L)
INR – 0.9	

Interviewer: What would your next course of action be?

Additional Scenario 6:

You are the IM Stage 1 doctor or call and have been asked to clerk a 35 year old woman who presents with acute shortness of breath and pleuritic chest pain. She denies any past medical history, with the exception of 3 miscarriages. Her HR is 82, her BP is 123/84, Sats 94%, RR 22 and Temp 36.8.

Interviewer: How would you approach this scenario?

Interviewer: Here are some of the investigation results: what is your interpretation of them?

RESULTS:

Hb – 132 g/L	(115 – 165 g/L)
WCC – 4.9 x10⁹/L	(4 – 11 x10⁹/L)
Plt – 369 x10⁹/L	(150 – 450 x10⁹/L)
Na – 137 mmol/L	(133 – 146 mmol/L)
K – 4.7 mmol/L	(3.5 – 5.3 mmol/L)
Ur – 4.2 mmol/L	(2.5 – 7.8 mmol/L)
Cr – 80 mmol/L	(59 – 104 mmol/L)
CRP – 14 mg/L	(<5 mg/L)
INR – 1.0	
Oxygen saturations – 91%	(94 – 98 %)
D-Dimer 280 ng/ml	(<230 ng/ml)

Interviewer: What would your next course of action be?

Additional Scenario 7:

A 28 year old woman has returned from travelling in Africa, and presents with headache, fever and shortness of breath. Her HR is 94, her BP is 109/65, Sats 97%, RR 19 and Temp 38.5. You are a member of the acute medical team, and have been asked to clerk this patient.

Interviewer: How would you approach this scenario?

Interviewer: Here are some of the investigation results: what is your interpretation of them?

RESULTS:

Hb – 107 g/L	(115 – 165 g/L)
WCC – 12.4 x10⁹/L	(4 – 11 x10⁹/L)
Plt – 190 x10⁹/L	(150 – 450 x10⁹/L)
Na – 139 mmol/L	(133 – 146 mmol/L)
K – 4.9 mmol/L	(3.5 – 5.3 mmol/L)
Ur – 3.2 mmol/L	(2.5 – 7.8 mmol/L)
Cr – 73 mmol/L	(59 – 104 mmol/L)
CRP – 63 mg/L	(<5 mg/L)

Interviewer: What would your next course of action be?

Additional Scenario 8:

A 53 year old gentleman presents with an acutely red, painful and swollen right first metatarsophalangeal joint. His HR is 68, his BP is 148/91, Sats 97%, RR 18 and Temp 37. You have been asked to assess this patient.

Interviewer: How would you approach this scenario?

Interviewer: Here are some of the investigation results: what is your interpretation of them?

RESULTS:

Hb – 167 g/L	*(130 – 180 g/L)*
WCC – 5.8 x10⁹/L	*(4 – 11 x10⁹/L)*
Plt – 228 x10⁹/L	*(150 – 450 x10⁹/L)*
Na – 139 mmol/L	*(133 – 146 mmol/L)*
K – 4.1 mmol/L	*(3.5 – 5.3 mmol/L)*
Ur – 4.5 mmol/L	*(2.5 – 7.8 mmol/L)*
Cr –73 mmol/L	*(59 – 104 mmol/L)*
CRP – 28 mg/L	*(<5 mg/L)*
INR – 1.0	

Interviewer: What would your next course of action be?

Additional Scenario 9:

An 82 year old female patient presents with a rash on her left lower limb, which started 4 days ago and has become hot and swollen. There is a small ulcer on the medial aspect of the area. Her HR is 85, her BP is 118/68, Sats 97%, RR 18 and Temp 38.1. You have been asked to clerk this patient as the IM Stage 1 doctor on call.

Interviewer: How would you approach this scenario?

Interviewer: Here are some of the investigation results: what is your interpretation of them?

RESULTS:

Hb – 113 g/L	*(115 – 165 g/L)*
WCC – 15.2 x10⁹/L	*(4 – 11 x10⁹/L)*
Plt – 231 x10⁹/L	*(150 – 450 x10⁹/L)*
Na – 135 mmol/L	*(133 – 146 mmol/L)*
K – 4.5 mmol/L	*(3.5 – 5.3 mmol/L)*
Ur – 9.3 mmol/L	*(2.5 – 7.8 mmol/L)*
Cr – 109 mmol/L	*(59 – 104 mmol/L)*
CRP – 83 mg/L	*(<5 mg/L)*

Interviewer: What would your next course of action be?

Additional Scenario 10:

You are the IM Stage 1 doctor on call and have been asked to clerk a 71 year old male. He presents with a 6 week history of weight loss, night sweats and intermittent fever. He has lost his appetite, and feels his strength is waning. There is mild left inguinal lymphadenopathy, and you note what you think is a large spleen. His HR is 66, his BP is 132/90, Sats 98%, RR 18 and Temp 37.

Interviewer: How would you approach this scenario?

Interviewer: Here are some of the investigation results: what is your interpretation of them?

RESULTS:

Hb – 120 g/L	*(130 – 180 g/L)*
WCC – 59 x10⁹/L	*(4 – 11 x10⁹/L)*
Plt – 159 x10⁹/L	*(150 – 450 x10⁹/L)*
Na – 137 mmol/L	*(133 – 146 mmol/L)*
K – 4.8 mmol/L	*(3.5 – 5.3 mmol/L)*
Ur – 5.9 mmol/L	*(2.5 – 7.8 mmol/L)*
Cr – 82 mmol/L	*(59 – 104 mmol/L)*
Corrected Ca – 2.7 mmol/L	*(2.2 – 2.6 mmol/L)*
CRP – <5 mg/L	*(<5 mg/L)*

Interviewer: What would your next course of action be?

Additional Scenario 11:

A 59 year old male smoker presents with haemoptysis for the past 7 days. This has never happened before and he is very concerned. His HR is 88, his BP is 138/89, Sats 96%, RR 20 and Temp 37. You, as part of the on call team, have been asked to review the patient.

Interviewer: How would you approach this scenario?

Interviewer: Here are some of the investigation results: what is your interpretation of them?

RESULTS:

Hb – 140 g/L	(130 – 180 g/L)
WCC – 5.8 x10⁹/L	(4 – 11 x10⁹/L)
Plt – 237 x10⁹/L	(150 – 450 x10⁹/L)
Na – 139 mmol/L	(133 – 146 mmol/L)
K – 4.5 mmol/L	(3.5 – 5.3 mmol/L)
Ur – 6.2 mmol/L	(2.5 – 7.8 mmol/L)
Cr – 78 mmol/L	(59 – 104 mmol/L)
CRP – <5 mg/L	(<5 mg/L)

Interviewer: What would your next course of action be?

Additional Scenario 12:

A 74 year old male patient presents with increasing shortness of breath and some weight gain over the last 2 months. He thinks that his ankles are more swollen than they used to be. He reports that his exercise tolerance has reduced significantly, and that he occasionally feels as if his chest is very tight, but denies palpitations and chest pain. His HR is 74, his BP is 151/94, Sats 96%, RR 22 and Temp 37. You are the IM stage 1 doctor on call and have been asked to clerk this patient in.

Interviewer: How would you approach this scenario?

Interviewer: Here are some of the investigation results: what is your interpretation of them?

RESULTS:

Hb – 129 g/L	(130 – 180 g/L)
WCC – 6.7 x10⁹/L	(4 – 11 x10⁹/L)
Plt – 209 x10⁹/L	(150 – 450 x10⁹/L)
Na – 142 mmol/L	(133 – 146 mmol/L)
K – 3.8 mmol/L	(3.5 – 5.3 mmol/L)
Ur – 6.1 mmol/L	(2.5 – 7.8 mmol/L)
Cr – 94 mmol/L	(59 – 104 mmol/L)
CRP – 3 mg/L	(<5 mg/L)
BNP – 381 pg/ml	(<100 pg/ml)

Interviewer: What would your next course of action be?

Example Scenarios: Answer Key

We provide here an answer key for the above Additional Scenarios. This ensures that you were on the correct path with your answers, and also illustrates some of the key points to make sure you cover if you are faced with any of these scenarios during the interview.

Additional Scenario 1:

➢ Consider causes of immunosuppression
➢ If considering Human Immunodeficiency Virus, think about diagnosis and think about ethical issues with contact tracing and confidentiality
➢ Consider the likely organism in the presentation of Acquired Immunodeficiency Syndrome (AIDS)
➢ Don't forget the likely AKI (consider all results given)

Additional Scenario 2:

➢ Diabetic Ketoacidosis
➢ Provide an explanation for all the results and how they contribute to your diagnosis
➢ Don't forget aggressive fluid rehydration as part of the treatment plan
➢ Follow local Trust's policy (see your intranet) on treatment with insulin

Additional Scenario 3:

➢ Likely gastroenteritis
➢ Consider potential causes, including viral
➢ May be prudent to send stool culture
➢ Don't forget all the bloods, patient's Urea & Electrolytes suggest she may be a little dry

Additional Scenario 4:

➢ Deep vein thrombosis as probable diagnosis – don't forget to calculate the Well's score prior to D-dimer
➢ Will require ultrasound Doppler
➢ Patient will require treatment with anticoagulation if you cannot arrange the Doppler scan on the same day
➢ Importance of exercise and raising leg to assist drainage

Additional Scenario 5:

➢ Possible infective endocarditis
➢ Consider different organisms and valves in intravenous drug users
➢ Know what your local empirical antibiotic choices would be
➢ Don't forget the 3 sets of cultures prior to antibiotic delivery
➢ Needs urgent echocardiography along with urgent cardiology review

Additional Scenario 6:

➢ Consider pulmonary embolism
➢ Again, perform Well's score
➢ Consider age of patient: will require pregnancy test before further investigation
➢ Consider recurrent miscarriages as possible clue to potential unifying diagnosis (anti-phospholipid syndrome)

Additional Scenario 7:

➢ Fever in returning traveller could be due to a number of causes, but important to consider malaria here
➢ Look at local policy: patient may require isolating
➢ Ask about anti-malarial prophylaxis
➢ Further investigation required includes blood film and cultures
➢ Referral to local infectious diseases unit

Additional Scenario 8:

➢ Have to rule out infected joint: septic arthritis is a medical emergency
➢ Additional tests: blood uric acid levels and ESR, x ray, and potentially joint aspiration if effusion present
➢ Consider treatment options, including colchicine and NSAIDs
➢ Referral to orthopaedics and rheumatology as required

Additional Scenario 9:

➢ Likely cellulitis
➢ Ensure patient not septic: ABCDE approach
➢ Swab ulcer for microbiology, be clinically of low risk of osteomyelitis or investigate further
➢ Empirical antibiotics (flucloxacillin)
➢ Don't forget all the bloods, patient's Urea & Electrolytes suggest she may have an AKI

Additional Scenario 10:

➢ Haematological malignancy: need breakdown of white blood cell count to confirm diagnosis
➢ Blood film required
➢ Ultrasound abdomen to confirm splenomegaly
➢ Haematology referral for likely bone marrow biopsy
➢ Treatment of hypercalcaemia

Additional Scenario 11:

- ➢ Urgent chest x ray required
- ➢ Lung cancer until proven otherwise
- ➢ Consider other differential diagnoses including tuberculosis, pneumonia and pulmonary embolism
- ➢ May have communication skills discussion about breaking bad news to the patient

Additional Scenario 12:

- ➢ May be the first presentation of heart failure
- ➢ Requires chest x ray and echocardiogram
- ➢ If fluid overload significant, then consider use of diuretics, but be careful of further derangements in urea and electrolytes

STATION 3: ETHICAL SCENARIO & PROFESSIONALISM

Station 3 represents an interview that is designed to test your aptitude in dealing with complex ethical and professional dilemmas. The station is usually divided into two sections: an ethical scenario, and a professionalism scenario; though as you will see in this chapter, the two stations are closely intertwined.

The **ethical scenario** may involve a complex discussion regarding the capacity of a patient to make a treatment decision. It may discuss difficulties in deciding what to do in patients with mental health conditions. The way to answer the scenario effectively is to ensure that you follow the underlying principles of Medical Ethics, and that you ensure that you always have the best interests of the patient at the centre of your argument.

The second component of this station is the **professionalism scenario**. This is designed to test your professional behaviour when put under a variety of different stressors. These scenarios may be very similar to situations you have already experienced as a junior doctor (for example, what to do when there is a sick patient but you need to leave work for a social engagement), and some will hopefully be lest familiar to the majority of applicants (for example, drunk colleagues).

We will first discuss some of the fundamental principles of medical ethics. We will then turn to sample scenarios and questions that may come up during the ethics scenario. Finally, we turn to a discussion of the professionalism station, and discuss examples that may come up.

Medical Ethics

Most of you will be familiar with the core principles of medical ethics, already having employed the principles throughout your training to date. If you desire a more formal refresher, then we would recommend reading *Medical Ethics: A Very Short Introduction* by Tony Hope, which gives a brief and accessible overview.

When presented with a question on medical ethics, it is essential to think about how the main principles of medical ethics apply.

The main principles of medical ethics are:

Beneficence

The wellbeing of the patient should be the doctor's first priority. In medicine, this means that one must act in the patient's best interests to ensure the best outcome is achieved for them, i.e. 'Do Good'.

Non-Maleficence

This is the principle of avoiding harm to the patient, keeping with the Hippocratic Oath "First do no harm". There can be a danger that in a willingness to treat, doctors can sometimes cause more harm to the patient than good. This can especially be the case with major interventions, such as chemotherapy or surgery. Where a course of action has both potential harms and potential benefits, non-maleficence must be balanced against beneficence.

Autonomy

The patient has the right to determine their own health care. This, therefore, requires the doctor to be a good communicator so that the patient is sufficiently informed to make their own decisions. 'Informed consent' is thus a vital precursor to any treatment. A doctor must respect a patient's refusal for treatment even if they think it is not the correct choice. Note that patients cannot demand treatment – only refuse it, e.g. an alcoholic patient, if deemed to have capacity, can refuse rehabilitation but cannot demand a liver transplant.

There are many situations where the application of autonomy can be quite complex, for example:
➤ **Treating children:** Consent is usually required from the parents, although the autonomy of the child is taken into account increasingly as they get older.
➤ **Treating adults without the _capacity_** to make important decisions. The first challenge with this is in assessing whether or not a patient has the capacity to make the decisions. Just because a patient has a mental illness does not necessarily mean that they lack the capacity to make decisions about their health care. Where patients do lack capacity, the power to make decisions is transferred to the next of kin (or Legal Power of Attorney, if one has been set up).

Justice

This deals with the fair distribution and allocation of healthcare resources for the population.

When answering a question on medical ethics, you need to ensure that you show an appreciation for the fact that there are often two sides of the argument. Where appropriate, you should outline both points of view and how they pertain to the main principles of medical ethics and then come to a reasoned judgement.

It is important to know that sometimes the beneficence and autonomy may be in conflict. For example, consider a patient that is refusing treatment that could be lifesaving. It is possible that sometimes the patients make decisions that are not correct or in conflict with beneficence duties of a doctor. When faced with such scenarios, try to understand the reasoning of the patient. Is it because of fear, ignorance or something different, for example religious beliefs. If the decisions of the patients are fully informed and the patient has the capacity to make well-informed decisions (patient is not confused due to illness/drugs or mental illness) then clinicians must respect the autonomy of the patient.

Further important **concepts in medical ethics** include:

Consent

This in a way is an extension of Autonomy: patients have the right to first agree (or refuse) to a procedure, treatment or intervention. For consent to be valid, it must be **a voluntary informed consent.** This means that the patient must have sufficient mental capacity to make the decision and must be presented with all the relevant information (benefits, side effects, and the likely complications) in a way they can understand.

Confidentiality

Patients expect that the information they reveal to doctors will be kept private. This is a key component in maintaining the trust between patients and doctors. You must ensure that patient details are kept confidential. This often comes up in scenarios where relatives may be asking for information about their parent who is a patient (has the patient given you permission to talk to their relative about their condition?) or if a patient/relative tries to have a discussion in the corridor (can you have the discussion in a more private area, less likely to be overheard?). Confidentiality can be broken if you suspect that a patient is a risk to themselves or to others, e.g. terrorism, child abuse, informing the DVLA if a patient is at risk of seizures, road accidents, etc.

Mental Capacity Act

The primary purpose of the 2005 act is to govern the decision-making process on behalf of adults who lack the capacity to make decisions for themselves. There are several principles to be aware of:

1. A person must be assumed to have capacity unless proven otherwise.
2. A person is not to be treated as unable to make a decision unless all practicable steps to help them to do so have been taken without success.
3. A person is not to be treated as unable to make a decision merely because they make an unwise decision.
4. An act must be in their best interest.
5. The act must be the least restrictive with regards to the individual's freedoms.

Capacity

Medical capacity arose from the Mental Capacity Act. It's the patient's ability to decide that they can make specific decisions about their care. The capacity is time and 'point' specific, meaning that they may not have the capacity to make complex financial decisions but can take decisions if they would like to have/decline specific treatment. This can change in time so there may be a time when they have capacity but other times when they don't (even within days or hours, depending on their clinical condition). For example, a patient admitted with a severe infection may not have capacity on their first day in hospital but this may change as they improve with treatment.

When assessing capacity, it is important to know that the individual does not have an underlying mental illness or a reason to compromise their decision-making abilities.

Important things to consider are:

➢ Can the patient understand the information?
➢ Can the patient retain the information?
➢ Can they analyse the information correctly?
➢ Can they communicate their choices clearly?

Any deficiency in any of these steps can lead to the patient lacking capacity to make a decision. The understanding of this process is crucial as doctors are often faced with situations where patients may make decisions that are not in keeping with medical advice (e.g. a Jehovah's Witness refusing blood products and having serious blood loss). Carrying out procedures or treatment that directly contravenes a patient's wishes who has capacity is a breach of patient's autonomy, and can be prosecuted.

Doctors should consider a formal mental capacity assessment in the following scenarios:

1. Sudden change in mental status
2. Refusal to treatment, e.g. unclear reason or due to irrational biases/beliefs
3. Known psychiatric/neurologic condition
4. People at extreme of ages < 18 years or > 85 years

Medical Law

Understanding the principles of medical law is also essential for success in this station. Here is a brief overview of some key legal cases and principles that you should familiarise yourself with:

Mental Health Act

This act basically governs how heath care professionals interact with people with mental disorders and their rights to force treatment. The original act was passed in 1983, but there was a significant amendment in 2007. The most significant components for health professionals are the definition of holding powers, which allow doctors to detain and treat a patient with a mental illness against their will. Most notably, these are the section 5(2) and 5(4) defining doctors' and nurses' duties respectively. Other orders to be aware off are Section 135 (magistrate order) and section 136 (police order), as well as section 2 and section 3 (detention for diagnosis and treatment, respectively). You should hopefully have covered these during your psychiatry rotations,

Data Protection Act

This act gives the GMC power to control how data is collected, recorded and used. Personal data under the act is defined as identifiable information. It's important that data is:

1) Processed fairly and lawfully
2) Gathered for specific purposes.
3) The data is adequate, relevant, accurate, and kept up to date

This governs how doctors collect patient information and who they can share this information with. Practical examples are doctors being allowed to break confidentiality for acts of suspected terrorism and road traffic accidents.

Gillick Competence

Children under the age of 18 can consent to treatment if they are able to understand, weigh up, and decide they want the treatment. However, they cannot refuse treatment until they are 18 years old. For children under 18 with no parent/guardian who aren't Gillick competent, you are able to act 'in their best interest'.

Bolam Test

The Bolam test is a legal rule that assesses the appropriateness of reasonable care in negligence cases involving a skilled professional. The Bolam test states *"If a doctor reaches the standard of a responsible body of medical opinion, he is not negligent"*. In order for someone to be shown to be negligent, it must be established that:
1) There was a duty of care
2) The duty of care was breached
3) The breach directly led to the patient being harmed

Euthanasia

Euthanasia is a deliberate intervention undertaken with the express intention of ending a life to alleviate pain and suffering. The two main types of euthanasia are:

➤ Active Euthanasia: Doctor causes the patient to die, e.g. by injecting poison
➤ Passive Euthanasia: Doctor lets the patient die, e.g. withdrawing life-sustaining treatment, switch off life-supporting machines

Active Euthanasia is classed as murder in the UK and is illegal. Passive euthanasia is legal. You should revise the main arguments for and against active euthanasia.

We now turn to a discussion of common ethical topics that frequently appear during the interview. We cover the main principles being asked in each scenario, and discuss the important things to cover in your answers.

Example Ethics Interview

SCENARIO: You are an IM Stage 1 doctor enjoying a well-earned Saturday shopping. You come across a patient you met and spent a good amount of time with on the Medical Assessment Unit after he was admitted with a first epileptic seizure. You are aware that his ex-wife was admitted at the same time. As the patient sees you, they wave and walk across the street to you. They reach into their wallet and pull out £100 to give to you.

Interviewer: *Welcome to the Station 3 interview. Have you had a chance to look at the scenario?*

Candidate: *Thank you, and yes I have indeed.*

Interviewer: *What would be your first action in this situation?*

Candidate: *I would acknowledge the extremely kind intentions of the patient, but I would explain that it would be unprofessional of me to accept their gift for doing my job and I would kindly request that they keep hold of their money.*

Interviewer: *The patient says I'll leave it on the street if you don't take it – what do you do now?*

Candidate: *I would again thank them for the kind thoughts, but would again explain that I cannot take it. I would suggest that if they feel strongly about giving a gift like this that they could consider donating this to a charity, but that it really wouldn't be necessary.*

Interviewer: *The patient then changes the topic of discussion. He believes that his ex-wife has been admitted to hospital, and moves closer to your ear and asks if you "know how she is doing?"*

Candidate: *I would explain that unfortunately I would be unable to divulge any information about his ex-wife's potential admission without her express permission prior to this. I would explain that I understand his concern, but I would not be doing my job properly if I were to break my duties of confidentiality.*

Interviewer: *The patient thanks you for your time, and moves to leave. He tells you that he is parked over the road, and is heading back to his car now. How would you act in this scenario?*

Candidate: *This is concerning to me because the patient clearly had a recent epileptic seizure, and therefore according to DVLA rules is not allowed to drive his car until further assessment and until he is at least 6 months seizure free. I would remind the patient of this case and explain that I am very sorry but he is not allowed to drive in this situation. I would suggest if he can that he has someone come to collect him and his car, and to attend follow-up as planned, aiming to begin driving again in 6 months.*

Interviewer: *Thank you, that completes Station 2. Good luck.*

Candidate: *Thank you for your time.*

Example Ethical Scenarios

1) A woman comes to you seeking an abortion. What do you do?

It is important to have some background knowledge as to the law regarding abortion as it is often the subject of ethical scenarios. Abortion is only legal in the UK under certain circumstances:

➢ If the child will suffer from a serious disability.
➢ If the birth is likely to cause serious physical harm to the mother.
➢ If the pregnancy is likely to in some way affect the mother's existing children.
➢ If the child/birth is likely to cause serious psychological harm to the mother.

The majority of abortions that are carried out are based on the last reason. If an abortion is being performed for the third or fourth reasons, it can only be done up to 24 weeks into pregnancy. There is no time limit if the abortion is being performed for the first two reasons. The partner also has no say in whether or not the abortion goes ahead. It is perfectly acceptable to object to abortion and not consent to carry out the procedure yourself – however, you are obliged to refer the woman to a colleague who can help her in your place.

A Bad Response:

I personally do not support abortion so I would tell the woman I would not be able to treat her. I would make sure she knows the consequences of what she is about to do and would make sure her partner knows. I would tell her to seriously reconsider undergoing the procedure.

Response Analysis:

The candidate is pushy in their personal opinion regarding abortion and is allowing this to influence the standard of care they are giving the patient, which is very unprofessional. Although it is of course fine to recommend that the patient tells the father if they are together, it is also a betrayal of the patient's trust to inform their partner in this instance, where they are not obliged to know as officially they have no say in the matter. The candidate has also shown no knowledge of what the law allows and is instead totally concerned with their opinion. They have also not recommended the patient to another colleague on refusing to treat them.

A Good Response:

First, I would make the patient feel comfortable, then talk to them about why exactly they want an abortion as it is a very serious procedure which they may regret later. I would also ask her if she is still with the child's father, and if so, whether or not he knows. I would recommend her telling him if they are still together. I would also find out how may weeks pregnant she is to see if she is still eligible for the procedure. As I myself object to abortion, I would refer her to my colleague, but I would make sure I didn't put this to her in a way that would make her feel ashamed or small. I would also assure her that I would keep being her doctor after the procedure and would make sure she had support in recovering from the procedure.

Response Analysis:

This is a very good answer. Many people will look at this question from a detached and objective point of view, forgetting the fact that you are theoretically talking to an *actual patient* who is thinking of undergoing a very serious procedure. Initially, establishing a rapport with the patient and finding out why they wish to have the procedure, as this candidate has done, is very important. Although the partner *officially* has no say, the candidate has rightly advised to inform them if relevant. This candidate objects to the procedure, which is perfectly fine, but has revealed this to the patient tactfully and has referred them to a colleague. The candidate could perhaps demonstrate more knowledge of the legal circumstances when an abortion can be done (otherwise, this may come in a follow-up question).

Overall:

Show some understanding of the law behind the matter, including when an abortion can be carried out and whether the partner needs to know. It is perfectly fine to object if you refer the patient to a colleague who can help her. As well as showing your knowledge of the legal side, make sure you show care and compassion to the mother during this difficult time.

2) You are in an outpatient clinic and a 16-year-old patient comes in, accompanied by her mother. You wish to speak to the patient alone as part of the consultation, however, the mother refuses to leave. What do you do about this?

When treating children, the majority of the time you will have to also communicate with their families and interact with them as they may play a key role in their care and decision-making. A question like this may be asked to test your ability to act politely but in the patient's best interest too. In medicine, you may be faced with difficult circumstances where you may be worried about being rude or offending someone, with both patients and relatives of patients. It is important to find a balance between being polite and also doing what you believe is right for the patient with their best interests in mind.

A Bad Response:

I would ask the patient what their own opinion would be, whether they would like their mother to leave the room or not. If the patient wishes for her mother to leave the room and her mother still does not comply, I would tell the mother that even if the mother refuses, her daughter has the right to be consulted alone and that I am suggesting this because I think it would be beneficial for the patient, in their best interest.

Response Analysis:

This answer is poor, firstly because it involves asking the young patient what they would want. Though this can be beneficial, if the patient is withholding information by saying they would like their parent to leave the room, it may draw attention to this, hence they may refrain from agreeing with their parent leaving. It may put the patient in an uncomfortable position. Also, the way in which the mother is dealt with, by forcing her to leave may create a bitter relationship with the family, especially if there are other children in the family and this may deter the mother from returning to the same GP.

A Good Response:

In a calm manner, I would suggest that according to standard protocol, I would like to see the patient alone. I would say that I am simply following protocol and this is not unusual with patients of this age and that I believe it is in their best interest. I would allow the mother to discuss her concerns with me about leaving the room and offer her the chance of also having a separate discussion afterwards (though I would ensure confidentiality is not broken) to allow her to discuss her own concerns about her daughter's health. To prevent this from happening again, I would begin my future consultations by telling patients of a specific age and their parents about the standard structure of consultations with a joint discussion to begin with, followed by a separate discussion with the patient and then with the parent alone should they wish.

Response Analysis:

This answer is much better as it shows the ability of the candidate to be polite whilst taking initiative and simply stating that it is standard protocol with patients of this age to be seen alone as well as with their parents, should they wish. Offering the mother a chance to be seen alone is also a good idea as it shows concern for both the patient and the parent. This answer finds a good balance between being polite and doing what you believe is right for the patient.

Overall:

In summary, when asked these types of questions, it is always important to demonstrate politeness and avoid actions that may damage rapport built between the patient/parent and the doctor. It is important to acknowledge that this is in the best interest of the patient and that no offence is intended to the parent.

3) A leukaemia patient is refusing stem cell treatment on religious grounds. Without the treatment, he has a 20% chance of survival. How would you use your communication skills to deal with this situation?

Paternalistic medicine (the attitude that the doctor always knows best) is falling out of favour. It's important to recognise that certain lifestyle decisions can be even more important to patients than their own health. It would be inappropriate to dismiss these choices even though the doctor's focus is on health. From a communication skills perspective, this question is asking you to demonstrate creativity in how you would use your own interpersonal skills to try to resolve the situation. Reaching a compromise between the patient's values and the physician's goals is a frequent conundrum in medicine, so being able to listen to the patient and figure out what is most important to them is an absolutely essential skill.

A Bad Response:
I would override his refusal by getting a court order as he clearly lacks the capacity to make a rational decision about his own care. Therefore, I should act in his best interests as I know from my medical training what is best for the patient, and it would be irresponsible of me not to do my best to treat him.

Response Analysis:
The response is poor and shows a lack of willingness to engage with the patient on his own terms. The court order is unlikely to lead to treatment being enforced either, especially if the patient has the capacity and is over 18. Whilst it is indeed true that doctors should try to do the right thing for their patients, this paternalistic view would be frowned upon in interviews as it makes the assumption that the treatment is what is best for the patient overall. This opinion suggests that the patient has a 'problem' to be 'fixed', rather than a complex combination of ideas, concerns, needs, and expectations. For example, this patient may suffer severe psychological distress from being forced to act against his beliefs. Therefore, is the stem cell treatment really the best option for his health?

A Good Response:
I would firstly try to understand the religious grounds behind his refusal. If there are conflicting opinions within his religion, it might be worth asking a religious representative (e.g. Chaplain or Rabbi) to visit him and discuss his options sensitively. If the patient is a minor and there is reason to believe he is being coerced rather than making his own decision, or the patient lacks capacity, there may be grounds for going to the court to get permission to treat him. However, at the end of the day, respect for patient autonomy must be paramount. If the patient has capacity and refuses the treatment, we must support his decision and instead treat any symptoms and problems he may have as a result of the refusal of treatment.

Response Analysis:
This is a good response. The first part demonstrates a desire to understand the patient's point of view, an open mind to learn about different cultures and backgrounds, and a willingness to use communication (even via a third party) to work through problems and issues. The second part demonstrates knowledge of the process of consent for minors, but interviewees wouldn't be expected to have an in-depth knowledge of the laws and processes involved in this. The third part of the response is the most important point – respect for the patient's decision also involves treating any problems they may have as a result of their (informed, consented) decisions. This is an essential aspect of medical care that many doctors struggle with.

Overall:
Being sensitive to the patient's motivations and concerns is an important part of being a doctor. This sort of question makes sure that the interviewee has the right attitude towards care that is expected of a modern doctor, and that they understand that 'acting in the patient's best interests' and giving the most efficacious treatment are not necessarily the same thing. It's also important to recognise that if a treatment is rejected, the doctor should give their best efforts to support the patient medically through other means, even if the patient experiences problems as a result of having rejected the therapy.

4) As a junior doctor you are called to an urgent situation. A patient is angry and is violently threatening the nursing staff. How might you calm this angry patient down?

This question focuses on how you can use your communication skills on the spot and under pressure to bring a difficult situation to a positive conclusion, and though relevant to the medical communications skills scenario, involves the key principles of medical ethics and so may appear in the Station 3 interview too.

A Bad Response:

There are several things that can be done to calm down an angry patient. Firstly, you could use communication techniques to show that you are not a threat. Secondly, you could use hospital security. Finally, you could explain to the patient that they should calm down as it will not benefit them to be angry. People often fail to realise that their anger only acts as a detriment to the care they might receive in hospital, so it is necessary to explain this to them.

Response Analysis:

This applicant's answer makes many faults. Firstly, the question asks you to put yourself into the situation, so it makes for a significantly stronger answer if it is delivered in the 1st person. Secondly, the points made are very weak. In questions that involve dealing with some kind of difficult patient, it is paramount that you put yourself in the patient's shoes and try and understand their emotions. Omitting to do this shows a lack of communication skills. In addition, this answer only talks in vague terms and doesn't describe what the applicant would actually do/say.

A Good Response:

The most important thing that must be achieved in this situation is to assess what is causing the patient to act in such a way. Is there something they are worried about? Something they are scared about? Or do they think that some kind of wrong has been done to them? Perhaps someone they care about, for example. To do this, it will be necessary to begin an effective dialogue with the patient. It is crucial that I give off a calm and confident persona both through speech and through body language. For similar reasons it is also key that the patient knows who I am, so I would be sure to introduce myself and explain why I had been called. For these reasons, I would begin by saying: "Hi, I'm Nicola, a junior doctor. I understand that there are a few things that you're not happy about. Could you tell me a little bit more about these so that I might be able to help?

I would make sure that I did not stand in a way that would block the exits and would check that the patient did not have some kind of weapon before I went any closer. If he did have a weapon, I would contact hospital security not only to ensure my own safety, but also for the safety of staff and patients. Upon initiating a dialogue, I would constantly remind the patient that we were there primarily to help the patient. After finding out the reason for the angry outburst, I would seek to solve this issue. I would keep in mind that the first concern that the patient raised might be something that was actually masking the real issue. I would also make sure to consider how the patient's autonomy might be being influenced by the treatment they were receiving."

Response Analysis:

This is a stronger answer. It covers all the key bases including; identifying the cause of the anger, identifying the need to protect yourself, and ensuring that you identify yourself to the patient. A strong answer should include all of these. Furthermore, the answer uses the first person and illustrates the points with a demonstration of what would actually be said, and identifies that a patient's autonomy (or an impingement thereof) can be a significant stressor in these circumstances.

Overall:

In questions like this, it's essential to demonstrate that you can put yourself in a patient's shoes and can think on the spot about how to deal with any situation that requires your communication skills.

5) What issues might arise when using a translator to mediate a patient consultation, and as a doctor, how might you overcome these issues?

This question asks about a part of medicine that is rarely discussed but is of increasing importance to clinical medicine in this country. 'Translators', in this case, could mean official in-hospital translators or could also include multilingual family members who are used for the purposes of translation. Make sure you define this in your answer.

A Bad Response:

It is bad to use a translator in a consultation. For example, the translator might not be able to translate things fully and so information will be missed. Also, time might be wasted trying to find the translator in the first place and this is especially important for busy doctors. There is a chance that the translator might not know medical terminology and so could struggle to relay all the correct information between the patient and doctor.

Response Analysis:

This is a terrible response for several reasons. Firstly, there is very little structure to the answer. The opening is weak, there is then a list of points that are poorly illustrated, and there is no conclusion that brings the points together at the end. Finally, this applicant has made the grave error of not answering both parts of the question. This is a mistake that is often made in the pressure of an interview setting. If you are in an interview and hear an 'and' that is joining two questions together, make sure in your head that you set out to answer both parts. You might structure this as two separate answers or combine answers to both into a single argument.

A Good Response:

In our increasingly multicultural society, the use of translators in medicine is increasingly prevalent and necessary. Many of the usual communication skills and techniques that are used by doctors are rendered useless when the patient does not speak the same language, and a strong patient-doctor relationship can be difficult to establish. Furthermore, in a profession in which strict confidentiality is essential, the use of unofficial translators may be open to abuse and any medical professional should do everything in their power to prevent such abuses.

There is a distinction between in-hospital official translators and when family members are used as translators, as is often the case in clinical medicine. A consultation that requires the use of a translator may not be ideal for either party, however, there are several things that the doctor might do to improve the situation. Firstly, before beginning the consultation, it is crucial that both the patient and translator understand the format of a translated consultation and are happy to proceed. This is especially true when a family member is used as a translator.

Secondly, it is key that all information is correctly conveyed across the language barrier. This can be achieved in several ways. For example, the doctor might use simple language and easily phrased questions. He/she should also only use short questions and wait for the translator to translate each portion. Finally, the doctor could regularly check and confirm throughout the consultation that the patient understands what is being said and indeed that the doctor has understood everything that the patient has said. Furthermore, there are several pitfalls that might occur during a consultation when using translators, and these pitfalls have the potential to be highly detrimental to the patient's welfare.

One potential issue is presented by the identity of the translator. If the translator is a family member or knows the patient personally, something which is quite likely if they come from the same community, then the patient might be embarrassed to present certain pieces of information that may be of critical importance to the consultation. In addition, the same could apply to the translator through their own embarrassment or ulterior motive. If any of these possibilities are suspected, then the doctor should seek to repeat the consultation with a different translator.

In summary, there are multiple important issues that arise through the use of translators in medicine. However, translators are an absolute necessity in our multicultural society, and therefore, doctors should be well educated on the possible pitfalls that might arise and should know how these can be avoided.

Response Analysis:
This applicant's answer starts with a strong opening that describes the importance of the issue. It then goes on to define what exactly the term 'translator' includes in this context. There is a strong structure with each point being well signposted. As opposed to having two separate answers to the two parts of the question, this applicant has decided to combine the two answers into one narrative. Either is acceptable.

Overall:
Always ensure you answer both parts of a question.

6) You are asked to gain consent from a patient for a procedure. What do you need to consider to ensure that consent is achieved?

As you gain experience throughout your career, you will be asked to take on more responsibilities. One of these responsibilities is taking consent for procedures: whilst you need to be careful that you are not asked to take consent inappropriately, the process of taking consent becomes much more relevant in IM due to the procedures that you will be performing (including intercostal drains and lumbar punctures).

A Bad Response:

Consent is very important in modern medicine; without consent, a procedure cannot go ahead. Consent is achieved when the doctor explains what the risks of a procedure are and has checked that the patient is happy to proceed. The issue of consent has many ethical implications. The Hippocratic Oath states that a doctor should do no harm and should act in the patient's best interests. Modern medicine relies on the fact that patients trust the medical profession to provide the very best service. If this trust is undermined, for example, by not following the Hippocratic Oath fully, then the medical profession cannot as effectively serve the population.

Response Analysis:

The key fault that this applicant makes in their answer is that they go off on a tangent about the ethical implications of consent. It is easy to fall into this trap as you may have a confident answer to something very much related to the question being asked, so it is tempting to talk about that even if it is not a direct answer. Always make sure that you structure a very relevant answer to the question that is being asked.

A Good Response:

Consent is a fundamental prerequisite of any procedure in an ethical healthcare system. Before visiting the patient, it is essential that you yourself understand the procedure, why it is being performed on this particular patient, and what the possible risks of the procedure are.

There are several key criteria that must be met to attain consent. Firstly, it is imperative to make sure that the patient fully understands what the procedure involves. For this reason, any explanation of the procedure given by the doctor should not involve medical jargon and should be at a level that the patient can comprehend.

Secondly, the patient must know about the risks involved. Even if a procedure is perfectly explained, this might imply that there aren't possible risks to the procedure and so the patient would not be able to give effective consent. Thirdly, the patient must know what the proposed benefits of the procedure are. Finally, it is crucial that the patient understands what will happen if they do not have the procedure. They may not wish to undertake a daunting procedure, but this might be by far the better of two options. Therefore, to be able to give true consent, it is necessary that the patient understands this.

However, before one can assess these different criteria, it is necessary to check that they can properly process information and that they can actually retain information. This could be done by asking the patient to repeat what you have said so far at various points during the consultation. Furthermore, we must give consideration to the patient's mental state, for instance, if they are not corpus mentis then consent cannot be obtained. This is because a patient who has a psychiatric condition may be able to appear to give consent but this cannot be accepted from an ethical standpoint.

Response Analysis:

The applicant gives an excellent answer to the question. There is a strong opening, followed by clearly structured key points that are a direct answer to the question. The applicant then goes into further detail by explaining pitfalls that could arise if we just followed the basic formula of consent.

Overall:

A key learning point in this example is to always make sure that you directly answer the question. This is a question about what informed consent is – not an ethical dilemma!

7) A patient is adamant that they will refuse your treatment and will instead use homeopathic medication. You believe that due to the seriousness of their condition, it is best that they follow your treatment plan. How might you go about doing this?

This question is not asking for an ethical argument (though the consideration of the four key ethical principles is essential), instead, it is questioning communication skills and techniques that would be used in the situation to reach the desired outcome for the patient.

A Bad Response:

I would make sure that I convinced the patient. To do this I would talk to them rationally and would set out in a logical manner why it was necessary for them to have my proposed treatment. I would also show that the benefits of the procedure would outweigh any possible risks.

Response Analysis:

This is a poorly answered question for several reasons. Firstly, most of the narrative is delivered in the first person (notice how there is lots of the use of 'I') and this creates a patronising outlook and shows that the candidate cannot put themselves in the patient's shoes. Furthermore, they have not considered what they would do in this scenario if the patient was still to refuse treatment. This is very important, as again, it shows that the candidate is not putting themselves in the patient's shoes and is not planning for different outcomes.

A Good Response:

A key pillar of the Hippocratic Oath is patient autonomy. However, if the practitioner strongly believes that a treatment that the patient will not consent to will give the best outcome, then it is his/her duty to try and persuade the patient of their preferred plan.

If I were the doctor in question, before going to the patient, I would read up on the case including the exact treatment option being declined as well as any alternative options. On seeing the patient, after building a rapport, I would try and assess the reasons for why the patient was refusing to accept the suggested treatment. Blunt logical reasoning is unlikely to be constructive in this type of scenario. It is important to show to the patient that I accept and register their beliefs. Simultaneously, I would be trying to assess whether they had an emotional reason as to why they might turn away from modern medicine. This might be an underlying fear or anxiety, or possibly even a previous bad experience.

Next, I would explain to the patient in the simplest language possible why I thought that their homeopathic treatment would not be effective and why the treatment that my team are proposing is going to be effective. I would then proceed to address the possible risks/benefits of the treatment and crucially explain why I thought the benefits outweighed the risks.

Finally, I would address any specific fears or bad memories that I felt the patient might have. It would be key throughout the whole consultation to ensure that I let the patient speak whenever they wanted to raise a point and that I was never overbearing, but instead, always courteous and understanding. I would hope that by doing this I could persuade the patient to accept the treatment. However, if the patient still refused to accept the treatment I would respect their wishes. I would also offer to arrange a second opinion to discuss this further.

Response Analysis:

This is a strong answer for several reasons. There is a strong opening set out for why it is an important situation. There are then several good points that are laid out in a structured manner and are well signposted. In addition, this candidate considers a plan B in case the patient still refuses treatment. Finally, this candidate has gone into extra depth to consider what might be driving this particular patient's beliefs.

Overall:

When answering a question such as this, always try and imagine yourself in the scenario as this helps you to consider what you'd have to say and also what other factors you might have to think about, for example, what to do if the patient continued to refuse treatment as these could be explored in follow-up questions.

8) You witness a doctor fill in a DNA-CPR with the patient, but without consulting with the patient's family. What issues do you see with this?

There are two main issues to consider. Firstly, how do DNARs work, and secondly, to what extent should a patient's family be involved in a decision that is primarily the concern of the doctor and patient.

A Bad Response:

This doctor is clearly breaching his professional obligations. End of life questions such as resuscitation orders always have to be discussed with the patient's family in order to make sure they adequately represent their wishes. Ignoring the family's wishes would be both unlawful as well as unethical. Every patient is entitled to all necessary treatments to maintain their life. This includes resuscitation at all cost.

Response Analysis:

Whilst this answer is in part right, it also has significant flaws. It is always preferable to consult with the family of a patient, especially when dealing with questions such as resuscitation, but ultimately the decision lies with the doctor as resuscitation is a treatment like every other. The decision to withhold or deliver treatment should be discussed with the patient, but once again, the ultimate decision lies with the doctor. In general, the doctor must always keep in mind the patient's best interest and this might include the decision to withhold resuscitation.

A Good Response:

If the patient wishes to discuss their end of life plans without involving their family, then the doctor has to accept this. Whilst ideally we would like to involve the patient's family, it is ultimately the patient's decision and ignoring this would represent a breach of confidentiality.

Response Analysis:

This is a good response as it delivers a short and succinct answer whilst acknowledging the finer points surrounding DNA-CPR. Remember that like with many ethical questions, there is no clear-cut correct answer.

Overall:

This is a challenging question with many both ethical and legal components. It's important to acknowledge the ethical challenges as you will almost certainly face them in your future medical career. It's important not to get carried away by your own opinions about end of life care. Not only will this impair the quality of the answer, it might also be misunderstood and reflect badly on you. Remember, medicine is not just about curing the ill – it is also about improving the quality of life of those we cannot cure.

9) A Jehovah's Witness is brought in by an ambulance to A&E after being in a road traffic accident and suffered massive blood loss. They need an urgent blood transfusion but the patient is refusing it. What do you do?

This is a classic ethical dilemma and variants on this frequently get asked. It's very important that you're aware of the law surrounding capacity and consent (see medical law section). The key here is to explore the patient's refusal for transfusion rather than falling into the trap of assuming that they don't want it as they are a Jehovah's Witness.

A Bad Response:

I would give the blood transfusion anyway because the first duty of the doctor is to do what is right for the patient. Therefore, if a blood transfusion is needed to save her life or prevents serious harm, then that would be best. This patient may not know what is best for them right now, but could be thankful after we give her the blood transfusion if it then saves their life

Response Analysis:

This response fails to consider the finer ethical and legal implications of transfusing someone against their wishes. There is no mention of patient autonomy or capacity. Nor does the response explore the reason for why the patient is refusing the transfusion.

A Good Response:

Initially, I would try to establish why the patient is refusing a blood transfusion – is it because they lack capacity? Or is it because of a phobia of blood products/needles? Or based on religious beliefs? There is a conflict in this situation between wanting to do what we, the healthcare professionals, perceive is in the patient's best interests, which is giving the blood transfusion and respecting the patient's autonomy. To balance these, I would first make sure that the patient understood the potential consequences of what could happen if they refuse the blood transfusion – including potential death. Also, I would check that they still have the mental capacity to make this decision, including asking about whether they have made a prior declaration about what they would want in this situation, and assessing whether they suffered a head injury in the RTA or could be delirious due to blood loss.

It would also be important to check that the patient is not under undue influence from any friends or family who are with them. If the patient seems to have full mental capacity, understand the consequences of their decision, and not appear to be under the influence of anyone else, then I would respect their wish not to have a blood transfusion while consulting with colleagues so that they can check my assessment of the situation. In addition, I would also explore alternatives to blood transfusion.

Response Analysis:

A fantastic response that gives a structured step-by-step guide as to what the applicant would do. They clearly have a sound grasp of the medico-legal implications and also avoid the trap of assuming the refusal is due to religious purposes.

Overall:

You might get asked follow-on questions of this theme, e.g. "Another unconscious patient is admitted following a car accident. They are believed to be a Jehovah's Witness. Would you transfuse?"

In this case, as the patient is unconscious I am able to act in his or her best interests and prescribe a blood transfusion, assuming there is no advance directive or family member preventing me from doing so (in which case, I would seek urgent legal advice).

A Jehovah's Witness with full capacity can refuse blood transfusion. However, in this situation it is possible they may have changed his or her mind, or became a Jehovah's Witness unwillingly.

10) You are treating a dictator who is responsible for the murder of thousands of people in his country. You are alone with him and realise killing him could save millions of lives. Assuming that you wouldn't get caught, would you do it?

As with any ethics question, the first thing to do is to recognise that there are **two sides to the argument** and to think about what these are. Ultimately, it matters less which side you choose (though for the sake of this scenario, it is fairly clear which side of the answer you need to come down on) than it does your ability to ethically justify your decision and the personal values you show in your argument. This is an opportunity to demonstrate a good understanding of relevant ethical principles and your ability to apply them practically. If there are potential flaws in your argument, it is much better to recognise them overtly than to try and gloss over them. Arguments of both sides should be given and then a reasoned decision on which is more powerful should be made.

A Bad Response:

I would never kill someone as it is murder and against the law, so I would definitely not kill the dictator. But maybe I just wouldn't treat him as well as I could and so hope that the disease kills him.

Response Analysis:

This candidate has failed to demonstrate the ability to use ethical reasoning to justify their decision or to show an understanding of any of the main tenants of medical ethics. They have also has not recognised that there could be another perspective on this problem and that arguments exist for killing the dictator. Finally, the suggestion of compromising care to the dictator certainly requires more justification. While it is true that there is an ethical difference between acts (killing the dictator) and omissions (failing to treat the dictator properly, in the hope he will die), this candidate does not really explain what they mean by this, and this comes across as very concerning from a professional standpoint.

A Good Response:

The arguments for killing the dictator seem reasonably clear – if doing so will save millions of lives then a utilitarian argument could state that this would achieve the best for the most people and so is the right decision, though there are a few problems with this. Firstly, you can't be sure of the assumption that killing the dictator will save lives – how do you know an equally bad dictator will not come through the ranks to take his place? Secondly, a murder by a medical professional completely breaks the implicit trust in universal beneficence to individuals and political impartiality that medical professionals rely upon to practice, especially organisations in conflict regions like MSF. If regimes stop trusting these organisations and allowing them to practice, it could be that more people are harmed than saved. Another strong argument against murdering the dictator is that it would be a clear violation of several cornerstones of medical ethics: respect for the sanctity of human life, non-maleficence and beneficence - the priority of the wellbeing of the patient in front of you, whoever they are. It is a slippery slope as soon as doctors start to judge whether or not the patients in front of them are worth helping. Ultimately, murder is fundamentally wrong in any situation. It is for these reasons and because you cannot even be sure of the utilitarian argument for killing the dictator that, on balance, I would not do so.

Response Analysis:

Although this response is quite long, such a difficult moral problem warrants a suitably thorough answer. This candidate clearly outlines ethical arguments for and against killing the dictator and then comes to a reasoned judgement. The candidate also shows a clear understanding of the concept of utilitarianism and knowledge of the principles of beneficence and non-maleficence, giving the interviewer the opportunity to ask more on those if they want.

Overall:

Notice that both the bad answer and the good answer came to the same conclusion: neither would kill the dictator. It was not the ultimate decision that was the difference between them, but rather their ability to reasonably justify their opinions with ethical argument and explain what they meant.

11) You're given £1 Million to spend on either an MRI machine or on 50 liver transplants for patients with alcoholic liver disease (cirrhosis). Which one would you choose?

Decisions about resource allocation are hugely important in a system like the NHS where resources are so limited and those making the decisions must be able to justify them to the public. Analysis of the cost-effectiveness of treatments is done by NICE, which assesses how money can be best spent to achieve the best for the most people. This uses measures such as QALYs (Quality Adjusted Life Years). The other ethical decision here is whether patients should be treated for arguably self-inflicted conditions.

A Bad Response:

I would pay for the MRI machine. This is because for the patients with alcoholic cirrhosis, their condition is self-inflicted and so they should be given less priority than patients whose diseases are not self-inflicted, like many of those who would be helped by the new MRI machine.

Response Analysis:

This alludes to a common ethical debate about whether, in a resource-limited public health system like the NHS, those with conditions which could be considered self-inflicted should be given less priority than other patients or perhaps be asked to pay for their healthcare. The arguments put forward for this include the idea that this would discourage people from unhealthy or risky lifestyle choices and so remove some of the burdens that these patients present to the NHS, while also benefitting the patients themselves. In contrast, arguments against this state that in many cases the causes of a disease can be multi-factorial, including lifestyle risk factors but also genetic predisposition for the disease, so it cannot be said with complete certainty that a person's lifestyle choices are responsible for the disease. Furthermore, such a move would represent a slippery slope towards doctors making dangerous judgements about which patients are worth treating and which are not. What makes this answer bad is that the candidate has failed to support their decision with an ethical argument or to recognise that their valid counter-arguments to his position. Furthermore, the candidate hasn't shown any awareness about how these resource allocation decisions are really made.

A Good Response:

I suppose my decision would have to depend on a number of factors. To start, I would want to know if there has been any analysis from NICE regarding which of these options has the potential to contribute to the most QALYs. While liver transplants make a relatively quantifiable improvement to the recipients' lives, it is difficult to quantify the amount of benefit from using an MRI machine – use of the machine does not generate QALYs in itself, but the earlier and more accurate diagnosis that it can offer certainly has the potential to do so. Another factor would, of course, have to be the relative need for MRI machines vs. liver transplants. For example, giving a hospital a second MRI machine will be of substantially more benefit than giving it its sixth MRI machine. Ultimately, I think this approach would probably lead me to opt for the MRI machine. This is because, although the liver transplants are of very obvious and substantial benefit to the 50 people who get the transplant, the MRI machine has the potential to last for decades and so help thousands of patients so that its cumulative contribution to wellbeing is perhaps greater.

Response Analysis:

This answer shows that the candidate has an idea about the process behind resource allocation decisions in the NHS and the role of NICE. It is also a thoughtful approach to the problems of working out how to fairly compare very different types of expenses, such as diagnostic tool versus a treatment. It is good that the candidate ultimately picks one of the options as the question explicitly asks for this and their choice is supported by the caveats that it would require deeper analysis and rely on an evidence-base.

Overall:

What matters more is not whether you pick the MRI machine or the liver transplants but your ability to give a balanced and rational ethical argument to support your answer, to demonstrate relevant knowledge and consider the practicalities of applying this in the real world.

12) What are the main principles of medical ethics? Which one is most important?

There are a few principles that are generally accepted as the core of medical ethics. It can be useful to read a little about them to make sure you have a good grasp on what they mean. See the Medical Ethics section for more details.

In answering this question, good answers will not just state what the main principles of medical ethics are, but why they are so important. You don't need to go into too much detail, just show that you know what the principles mean. In choosing which principle is most important, it is good to show balanced reasoning in your answer, i.e. that you recognise that any single one of the principles could be argued to be the most important but for specific reasons you have picked this one.

A Bad Response:

It is really important for doctors to empathise with their patients, so empathy is probably the main principle. If doctors empathise with their patients, this means they will do what is in the patients' best interests, so it is the most important principle in medical ethics.

Response Analysis:

Empathy is obviously an important component of the doctor-patient relationship and the ability to empathise is crucial for all medical professionals, but it is in itself not a principle of medical ethics. The candidate seems to be getting at the idea of beneficence but does not really explain what they mean or why it is so important. If you are asked to make a judgement on which medical principle is most important, it is a good idea to have mentioned other medical principles earlier in your answer to compare it to. Thus the main way in which this answer falls down is in having shown no real appreciation for so many of the medical principles mentioned above.

A Good Response:

The main principles of medical ethics are usually said to be beneficence, non-maleficence, autonomy and justice. It is very difficult to say which is most important as, by definition, they are each crucial in medicine and they are all very linked with each other. For example, if a patient wants a treatment that a resource-limited health system, like the NHS, can't offer without compromising the healthcare to someone else then this is a conflict between autonomy and justice. If I had to pick, I would say that beneficence is probably the most important principle as if it is applied to all your patients then it should imply justice and if a patient is properly respected, then it should also take into account the importance of autonomy.

Response Analysis:

This candidate showed knowledge in both the main principles and understanding of what they mean and how they could be applied practically. Notice how this candidate showed their understanding without actually defining each principle, though there wouldn't necessarily have been anything wrong with doing so. This candidate recognised the difficulty in picking a 'most important' principle, in so doing showing balance and humility. Their insight into the conflict between different principles further shows a good understanding and suggests they have given medical ethics a good degree of thought.

Overall:

This question can be a really easy one if you familiarise yourself with the main principles of medical ethics so that you know you can define them and recognise how they might apply in a clinical setting. The question of which is 'most important' has no single right answer – it can be good to say this and then make sure you have a reasonable justification for whichever principle you pick.

13) What do you understand by "confidentiality"?

Confidentiality is a legal obligation and an ethical obligation (required by professional codes of conduct). It means not sharing information about patients without their consent and ensuring that written and electronic information cannot be accessed or read by people not involved in the patient's care. Informed consent and patient capacity are considered essential in maintaining the privacy of the patient. Confidential data is any information that could be used to identify the patient; this includes name, address, etc.

Confidentiality is important for several reasons. One of the most important elements of confidentiality is that it helps to build and develop trust. Patients may not trust a healthcare worker who does not keep information confidential and we know that trust is key to a doctor-patient relationship. A client's safety may be put at risk of discrimination and stigma if details of their health are shared publicly, e.g. a HIV diagnosis.

Discussions about the patient should take place in the workplace and not be overheard to general public. To ensure confidentiality, information should only be disclosed to third parties (such as another government agency or a family member/carer) where a patient has consented to the release of the information. Further workers need to ensure that any information that is collected is securely stored and disposed of.

There are few exceptions to the general rule of confidentiality and they all have legal bases. These include, but are not limited to: if a serious crime has been committed; if the client is a child and is being abused/at risk of abuse; or if you are concerned that the client might harm someone else. When legal obligations override a client's right to confidentiality, there is a responsibility to inform the patient and explain the limits of confidentiality.

A Bad Response:
Confidentiality is what prevents us from sharing patient information with others. It means that we cannot talk about patients in open places in case others overhear.

Response Analysis:
The response itself is correct and contains all true information but it is lacking in detail. Using the word "cannot" implies that the candidate does not understand the ethical obligation; it would be better to use "should not". This answer does not discuss the importance of confidentiality and how it gives patients the confidence to disclose. It also doesn't address the limitations of confidentiality and scenarios when it can be breached.

A Good Response:
Confidentiality is the legal right of the patient to not have their information disclosed to outside parties. Patients entrust us with sensitive information relating to their health and other matters when they seek treatment so we also have an ethical obligation to keep confidentiality. Patients share in confidence and help build the patient-doctor relationship. There are also some circumstances where confidentiality may be breached. These can include notifiable diseases and cooperation with social services or when a crime is involved.

Response Analysis:
This answer has a clear definition of confidentiality and mentions the ethical obligation healthcare workers have to keep confidentiality. This candidate clearly understands the importance of patient trust and how it affects the patient-doctor relationship. They also discuss the conditions in which we can breach confidentiality, which shows that the candidate has a great understanding of the issue.

Overall:
A good answer will clearly define confidentiality and discuss its importance with "patient trust" as a buzzword. It will also discuss the conditions in which confidentiality may be broken.

14) When can doctors break confidentiality?

As doctors, we have an ethical & legal obligation to protect patient information. This improves patient-doctor trust. However, there are circumstances when doctors are required to break patient confidentiality, such as:

➢ The patient is very likely to cause harm to others, e.g. mental health disorder
➢ Patient doesn't have the capacity, e.g. infants
➢ Social Service input is required, e.g. child abuse
➢ At request of police, e.g. if a patient is suspected of terrorism
➢ Inability to safely operate a motor vehicle, e.g. epilepsy
➢ Notifiable diseases

A Bad Response:

Doctors can break confidentiality when they believe that it will benefit the patient. Confidentiality is an important aspect of medical care because it protects patients from having information that is private to them being disclosed to the public. Confidentiality can also immediately be broken if a patient who has been advised not to drive is found to be driving as it causes a risk to the public if the driver is involved in an accident.

Response Analysis:

The first sentence in this response is a little vague; ideally, the candidate would expand on how exactly breaking confidentiality would benefit the patient. For example, is it because the patient in question is in grave danger from abuse, threatened by a weapon, or details about them need to be disclosed in order to catch the criminal? The question does, however, appreciate the importance of maintaining confidentiality. To state that confidentiality can be broken immediately without first consulting the patient (as in the driving scenario) and advising them of disclosing information themselves is technically inaccurate.

A Good Response:

Patients have a right to expect their doctors to maintain confidentiality and doing so is very important to maintain a good patient-doctor relationship as well as maintain the public's trust in the profession. However, there are a number of circumstances under which doctors may break confidentiality. As stated in the GMC guidance, it may be broken if it is required by the law, if it is in the public's best interest due to a communicable disease such as Measles (also required, as this is a notifiable disease) or a serious crime needing to be reported such as a gunshot wound. It is always important to ask patients first if their information can be disclosed and to encourage them to disclose things themselves. For example, if a person with uncontrolled epilepsy is driving, you have a duty to report it to the DVLA but you must give the patient every chance to tell the DVLA about their condition themselves. In this case, you can only break confidentiality if the patient refuses to inform the DVLA so that you can protect them and the general public.

Response Analysis:

The response identifies the importance of maintaining confidentiality. The candidate nicely references an appropriate source for doctors such as the GMC to state instances in which confidentiality is broken. This shows that the candidate has read the guidance that doctors are expected to know and is able to apply their knowledge to answer this question. The examples are accurate.

Overall:

It is important to be familiar with key 'hot topics' in medicine such as consent and confidentiality and to carry out a little background reading on these prior to attending a medical interview in order to provide them with accurate examples. Examiners will indeed be impressed if you understand these core concepts and their importance to medical practice. The GMC website's 'good medical practice' is a very good site to visit in order to obtain further information on these topics and others that are likely to be assessed in your interviews.

15) Do you think people injured doing extreme sports should be treated by the NHS?

The crux of this question comes from the implication that those who do extreme sports, such as skydiving, are people who voluntarily take risks with their health and should not expect taxpayers to pay for their medical care if they are injured. This is reflected in a private healthcare where people who take risks would have to pay a higher fee. Patients often argue that they have the right to healthcare since they themselves are taxpayers and by paying to support others they also have the right to seek treatment.

We can analyse this question with the principle of justice because healthcare systems, such as the NHS, have limited resources so we must place restrictions on how funds are spent. It would release funds that could be spent on others who have not purposefully put themselves in harm's way. However, the principle of autonomy also plays a role; a person's autonomy has to be respected. They have a right to decide how to live their life and participate in extreme sports if they wish. Looking at a third principle, beneficence, it is important to be non-judgemental and act in the best interests of the patient, which means treating injuries. Most medical professionals will prioritise the principles of autonomy and beneficence over justice.

We can draw a parallel between the situation proposed and denying treatment to those who are ill due to lifestyle choices. These conditions are often seen as "self-inflicted" and include smoking- or obesity-related diseases. If we begin excluding those who participate in extreme sports, it is a slippery slope before we exclude lifestyle diseases from public funded treatment.

A Bad Response:

People who do extreme sports put themselves at risk; their injuries can be avoided by simply following a different lifestyle. This is not fair to others who are leading normal lives. However, people who do extreme sports also pay taxes which contributes to the running of the NHS so they are entitled to use it.

Response Analysis:

The response is good because it shows a balanced view. However, it misses the opportunity to get into detail. For example, they did not discuss patient autonomy and the patient's right to lead their life as they see fit. Doctors can give advice but should not penalise them for not following it. Another ethical principle that was not fully discussed is justice. The NHS has limited resources so should we redistribute our funds to only people who cannot avoid their injuries? Another fault with this answer is that it misses the key connection between the question and the treatment of alcoholics and smokers with a self-inflicted disease.

A Good Response:

The NHS is a publicly funded institution and for the general public. We should not limit anyone's access to it. This goes against the principle of non-maleficence. Others may argue that people doing extreme sports are causing themselves avoidable harm and their injuries are self-inflicted so the NHS funds could be better spent elsewhere – thus following the principle of justice. However, this is analogous to the treatment of alcoholics and smokers. We treat such people within the NHS because the service is for the promotion of better health (beneficence) so it is not ethical to withhold treatment.

Response Analysis:

This answer starts with a strong opinion and gets straight to the point – this will catch the interviewer's attention. This is then followed by a balanced argument showing the candidate is able to consider opposing opinions. Drawing a parallel between the question and the treatment of other lifestyle diseases is essential in an excellent answer. Being able to refer to current topics or issues in the NHS is the sign of an excellent candidate. This answer also discusses all the ethical principles apart from autonomy – the answer would be improved if autonomy was also used.

Overall:

When answering an ethical question, use the ethical principles (autonomy, beneficence, non-maleficence and justice) to structure your answer. Giving a balanced view also shows you understand both sides of the argument and makes you stand out as a strong candidate.

16) Should the NHS fund IVF? What about injuries that arise from extreme sports such as mountain climbing?

This question essentially addresses two different subjects, both relating to a similar basic issue: shortness of funds. Since we're in the UK and are arguing on the background of the tax-funded NHS, the basic question is how far society can be held responsible for covering the costs of treatment resulting from the actions of individuals.

A Bad Response:

The NHS should fund neither IVF nor health care for extreme sports injuries. IVF is a service that is hugely expensive and has a fairly low success rate. Funding cycle after cycle of IVF is just not sustainable and at some point, the patient has to accept that they just cannot get pregnant – especially if the difficulties are simply due to the mother putting her career first and now being too old to conceive. There are plenty of children looking to be adopted. The same applies for injuries resulting from extreme sports. It is unacceptable for society to pay the bill for when somebody's hobby goes wrong. If individuals believe that they need to go mountain climbing and get hurt in the process, it is up to them to cover the bill, not society. The NHS just does not have the funds for this.

Response Analysis:

This response is judgemental and shows very little understanding of what the NHS is about and, more importantly, what it means to be a doctor. The idea of the NHS is to provide healthcare for everybody – indiscriminate of their income and social class and that includes support with conception. In addition, there are tight regulations in place when it comes to cyclic treatments such as IVF, where 2 cycles are covered by the NHS and all further cycles have to be covered by the patient. In regards to the extreme sports, this answer shows great ignorance with regards to a doctor's duty of care. Whilst it can be argued that extreme sports-associated injuries are the individual's fault, what about diseases associated with smoking and alcohol, poor diet or even simple activities such as driving? These can just as easily be attributed to individuals and cost the NHS much more money than extreme sports.

A Good Response:

This is a very complex question. It addresses the question of what treatments are affordable and logical in times of shortening funds. Instead of focussing on these two very specific examples, this question should be approached on a more general level. In principle, the NHS is based on the idea that everybody living in the UK should have access to healthcare. This includes treatments for infertility as well as for injuries associated with extreme sports. The most fundamental idea of the NHS is to not differentiate between diseases themselves but to ensure that everybody gets treatment. Unfortunately, during times of shortening funds, there need to be limits to this as some modern treatments are very expensive. It is for that reason that in IVF, for example, only a limited number of cycles is NHS-funded. On a more doctor-centred level, being non-judgmental is of central importance. It is our duty to treat everybody, irrespective of race, creed, gender or the cause of their injury or disease.

Response Analysis:

This is a good response as it acknowledges the complexity of the issue whilst relating it back to the specific question. It is non-judgemental in that it does not assign blame and tries to address the root cause of the problem. For a good response, it is important to provide a differentiated and logical answer that does not fall victim to personal opinions or rash impulses.

Overall:

Medical Ethics is rarely ever black or white: there are always grey areas. The main challenge of this question is to avoid rash and sweeping statements and to answer in an undifferentiated manner. The IVF part of the question is a particularly difficult subject, mostly because it is very difficult to assign responsibility for the inability to conceive. The mountain climbing part is somewhat less challenging as blame is assigned more easily. Be careful, though, as it is very easy to fall into the blame trap.

17) Why is euthanasia such a controversial topic?

Euthanasia is a topic that comes up a lot in many ethical discussions in medicine. It is a very controversial topic as the definition of euthanasia itself is a complicated one and it also stands in fundamental conflict with what it means to be a doctor: to preserve life.

A Bad Response:

Euthanasia describes the medical killing of people. It can be seen as controversial as the bottom line is that it is murder to end a life. In euthanasia, a doctor kills his patient because the patient's life is considered not worth living and he (the patient) would be better off being dead. In that sense, it represents the most merciful step to take.

Response Analysis:

This is a bad response as it is too undifferentiated for an issue as complex as euthanasia. The question asks about the controversy surrounding it and this is in part due to the very nature of euthanasia. Whilst the above answer superficially touches on these issues, it does not explore the issue sufficiently to be an appropriate answer. Be aware of how complex the matter is and do not trivialise it.

A Good Response:

Euthanasia is a controversial topic for a multitude of reasons that come from a variety of different backgrounds. One of the reasons for controversy lies in the very definition of euthanasia. Euthanasia is defined as the ending of life to alleviate suffering. This almost makes it sound like a form of treatment. The controversy arises when one considers the very meaning of being a doctor. It is the doctor's duty to safeguard and protect life, not to end it. On the other hand, the idea of duty of care and patient well-being is the very thing that may justify the ending of life to alleviate suffering. In essence, the controversy on an ethical level arises in part from the conflict between safeguarding life and ending it to reduce suffering.

Other causes for controversy lie in issues such as communication where the question is asked how, for example, a comatose or paralysed patient can communicate their wish to live or die. A further point to take into consideration is the idea of life not worth living. Once we accept that there is a life that can be declared as not worth living, where does that lead us? Some fear that it will lead to a slippery slope where definitions of unworthy life become increasingly arbitrary.

The GMC code of good medical practice and UK law currently don't permit euthanasia.

Response Analysis:

This is a good answer as it directly addresses the complexity of the issue and then attempts to provide explanations and examples for the different issues. The answer also attempts to demonstrate the controversy in that it provides the point of view of the two main camps involved in the discussion. This is important as only with opposing opinions can there be controversy.

Overall:

This question is a challenging one as it is easy to get lost in one's own opinion. It is important to have a correct definition of euthanasia as it is very easy to answer this type of question wrong if the definition is incorrect. Whilst one has to be careful with one's own opinion, it provides a good starting point as it will allow for examples and arguments of both sides.

18) What is the difference between euthanasia and physician-assisted suicide?

Background Analysis:
Euthanasia is the act of deliberately ending a person's life to relieve suffering. Assisted suicide is the act of deliberately assisting or encouraging another person to kill themselves. In a practical example, a doctor administering a patient with a lethal injection to stop their suffering would be euthanasia. If the doctor handed the lethal injection to the patient so they injected it themselves, this would be physician-assisted suicide. The best answers to this question will go beyond knowing the different definitions to being able to interpret what implications these definitions have on the differences between euthanasia and physician-assisted suicide legally and ethically.

A Bad Response:
Aren't they basically the same thing? It means when a doctor helps someone who is seriously ill to die so that they are not in any more pain. I know it is illegal and I think maybe that when it is counted as murder, then it is euthanasia and when it's counted as manslaughter then it is called physician-assisted suicide.

Response Analysis:
This is clearly wrong. In an answer like this, it is better to simply admit it if you don't know what the definitions of these terms are, instead of trying to guess them.

A Good Response:
The difference between euthanasia and physician-assisted dying is that in the former, the doctor is actually doing the act that kills the patient, whereas, in the latter, the doctor is merely assisting the patient to kill themselves. There are several important differences between the two. For example, in physician-assisted suicide, the patient's desire to die is, by definition, a requirement. This is not necessarily the case for euthanasia, which can be voluntary, non-voluntary or involuntary. It is because of this that some people argue that physician-assisted suicide is more morally acceptable because it is in accordance with patient autonomy whereas euthanasia is not necessarily. However, it is sometimes argued that this discriminates against those who are too disabled to commit suicide, even with physician-assistance, and that in these cases, active voluntary euthanasia should be allowed as ultimately the intention is the same. Legally, there is also a big difference – active euthanasia is regarded as murder or manslaughter whereas physician-assisted dying is not, though it is still illegal.

Response Analysis:
This answer shows good knowledge of the definitions of euthanasia and physician-assisted suicide, as well as the different types of euthanasia. It shows an appreciation for the ethical distinction between the two and some of the controversy that surrounds the issue. It is always a good idea to include ethical principles like autonomy in your answer. The candidate could perhaps do more to explain whether they think there is an ethical difference between physician-assisted suicide and active voluntary euthanasia.

Overall:
These distinctions are of huge importance in medicine and are the source of much debate and controversy, so it is worth familiarising yourself with them now. The best answers will demonstrate not only knowledge of these concepts but also an understanding of what they mean and how ethical arguments tie into them.

19) Discuss the ethical dilemma of Huntingdon's disease when one family member knows they have it and don't want anyone else to know.

Huntington's disease is a devastating neurodegenerative disease with no cure; it affects the coordination of movement and leads to mental decline. The diagnosis is usually confirmed by genetic testing and affected individuals show disease progression in a predictable way. The genetic testing can even predict when symptoms will begin to affect the individual. In the latter stages of the disease, sufferers require full-time care, which often affects life for the surrounding family. The disease is inherited in an autosomal dominant fashion which means offspring have a 50% chance of developing the disease, however, it should be noted that individuals suffering from the disease often choose not to have children because of this risk. There are a wide range of ethical issues that arise from the diagnosis of Huntington's disease and they will be explored in more detail in the answers below. When approaching ethical questions like this, the key thing is to explain your reasoning for your thought and to discuss both sides of the argument. Ensure you answer the question too, explain why this is a 'dilemma'.

A Bad Response:
Huntington's disease is a devastating neurodegenerative disease that develops predictably, and sufferers require full-time care in the latter stages of the disease. This is likely to put significant pressure on close family and friends. Importantly, the disease is inherited in an autosomal dominant pattern, which means that any offspring have a 50% chance of suffering from the disease. For both of these reasons, it would be wrong for a sufferer of the disease to keep it a secret from their family and partner. Family deserve to know that their relative is certain to require care later in life and details about the potential effect on offspring should not be kept from a partner. It is, therefore, the GP's duty to inform the family and partner in a situation where the individual with the disease does not wish to share their diagnosis.

Response Analysis:
This answer raises two of the important ethical dilemmas surrounding a diagnosis of Huntington's. The progress of the disease is devastating and sufferers will come to require full-time care. This is something that families understandably would like to prepare for however many sufferers do not want this sense of impending doom hanging over their family's heads and would rather break the news later. Similarly, when it comes to reproduction some couples would like to undertake IVF and use pre-implantation genetic testing to ensure an embryo with HD will not be used for reproduction but there are individuals who feel this is morally wrong and so may prefer to keep their diagnosis a secret from their partner. Whilst the answer raises these two points, it doesn't discuss why an individual may not want to share their diagnosis. The question asks about the ethical dilemma so both sides of the argument should be offered. The answer also incorrectly states that it is the GP's duty to inform the family and partner. This would be a breach of confidentiality; the GP can only encourage the patient to share this information with their family.

A Good Response:
Huntington's disease is a devastating neurodegenerative disease which develops predictably and sufferers require full-time care in the latter stages of the disease. Genetic testing can predict when symptoms will begin to appear which can be very stressful for sufferers. An individual diagnosed with HD may not wish to share this information with their family for a number of reasons. The disease is inherited in an autosomal dominant pattern which means each of the sufferer's offspring has a 50% chance of being a sufferer and also that at least one of the sufferer's parents will also suffer. Since this disease does not have a cure, some say it is unethical to inform people that they will develop this disease long before they ever develop symptoms.

However, others argue that knowledge that the disease will progress allows patients to plan their lives. Other important factors to consider are the ages of family members, some members may be too young to be tested because they may not be deemed mature enough to deal with news of a diagnosis. Individuals may also hide this information from family for financial reasons. If family members are aware of the diagnosis and get tested themselves to discover they too have HD, they will be required to pay much higher costs for medical insurance.

Whilst one can argue that individuals can access free healthcare on the NHS, often the provision of care for individuals with debilitating chronic conditions can benefit from extra help beyond what the NHS provides, and therefore health insurance is an important safety net. In addition, I would be unable to inform the family myself due to confidentiality but I would stress that it is important that everyone in the family should have the opportunity to think about their long-term plans should they have HD or if they will end up caring for someone with HD.

Response Analysis:

This is an excellent response which really explains why this is a dilemma for a patient. It gives both insightful reasons why a patient may want to keep the diagnosis a secret but also offers the conflicting thoughts that a patient may have in weighing up a decision to tell someone. Finishing the answer by stating what the candidate would do as the patient's doctor helps this answer to stand out.

Overall:

In any ethical question, ensure you provide a balanced argument but try to come to a conclusion if you can. You will get extra credit if you can understand how doctors fit into these situations and can demonstrate knowledge of legal issues limiting doctors' actions e.g. confidentiality.

Professionalism Scenario

The professionalism scenario is often interlinked with the ethical scenario, but for the purposes of this book we will discuss them separately to ensure that the core principles that need to be covered in each are not missed.

The most important guiding principle in the professionalism scenario is that you must aim to prevent patient harm, and therefore protect patient safety, at all costs. This means that the most important focus of your answer will be to ensure that your actions safeguard the health of patients: whether this means removing drunk colleagues from clinical areas, or staying late to ensure appropriate handover of a sick patient.

Following establishment of how you would act to preserve patient safety, you then dissect the rest of the case and discuss how you would act as a professional in each situation. Think back to the Situational Judgement Test: the principles you applied there are exactly the same as you need to apply here.

Situational Judgment: A Refresher

The Situational Judgement Test assessed your ability to prioritise competing demands and resolve disputes in a harmonious manner.

When faced with a situational question, it is helpful to use a basic framework:
1. Identify the basic dilemma
2. Identify your potential courses of action
3. Consider the advantages & disadvantages of each option you're given
4. Consider any alternative solutions, i.e. options outside the ones you are given
5. Think about how the perspectives of colleagues and patients may differ from your own
6. Balance these to pick an action that you can justify with a logical argument

Read "Tomorrow's Doctors" and "Good Medical Practice"

These are publications produced by the General Medical Council (GMC) which can be found on their website. The GMC regulate the medical profession to ensure that standards remain high. These publications can be found on their website. Reading through this ensures you have the required principles at the forefront of your answers.

Hierarchy

The patient is of **primary importance**. All decisions that affect patient care should be made to benefit the patient. Of **secondary importance** are your work colleagues. So if there is no risk to patients, you should help out your colleagues and avoid doing anything that would undermine them or harm their reputation – but if doing so would bring detriment to any patient, then the patient's priorities come to the top. Finally, of **lowest importance** is yourself. You should avoid working outside hours and strive to further your education, but not at the expense of patients or your colleagues.

There are several core principles that you should attempt to apply to SJT questions that will help your decision making:

Adopt a Patient-Centred Approach to Care

This involves being able to treat patients as individuals and respecting their decisions. You should also respect a patient's right to confidentiality unless there is a significant risk to the general public. The most important principle is to **never compromise patient safety**.

Working Well in a Team

Teamwork is an essential part of any job. You must be a trustworthy and reliable team member and also communicate effectively within the team. You should support your senior and junior colleagues should they require it. It is important to avoid conflict and be able to de-escalate situations without jeopardising professional relationships where possible.

Commitment to Professionalism

You should always act with honesty and integrity as this is expected of anyone entering the profession. This includes apologising for your mistakes and trying to ensure other people apologise for theirs.

Taking Responsibility for your learning

Medicine is a career where you are continuously learning. You are the sole person responsible for it and you will need to prioritise your jobs to ensure you attend scheduled teaching and courses. You should be able to critically reflect upon your experiences.

Example Situational Judgement Questions

Example A:

"The ward nurse informs you that one of your FY1 colleagues is taking lots of morphine from the drug cabinet. What do you do?"

This question is not about your knowledge of morphine but about what to do if someone you know is reported to be doing something that is not correct. The obvious trap here is to say, *"I would go speak to the doctor and inform their boss."*

This would be a very serious accusation; remember that the nurse may be wrongly informed, biased or have a grudge against that doctor. Before you do anything, you must show that you will find out the facts and establish whether this is a recurring problem or not and if there are any obvious explainable reasons for it.

Thus, although the question might appear to be very simple, it actually tests multiple skills. It's important to consider the implications of your actions rather than launch into an answer straight away.

"Reports of a colleague taking medication from a patient's drug cabinet is clearly extremely concerning. Before I do anything, I would try to establish the facts by talking to others who may be in a position to observe such behaviour. This will ensure that it removes any reporter's personal bias or perceptions. If this is true, I would offer to speak to the colleague in private and ask their views. I would offer my support by covering their work to ensure that patient safety is not compromised, and would ask them to leave the clinical area and talk to their educational supervisor as a matter of urgency. I would encourage them to get external help, and I would involve my seniors if I felt that the situation wasn't resolving."

Example B:

You are just finishing a busy shift on the Acute Assessment Unit (AAU). Your FY1 colleague who is due to replace you for the evening shift leaves a message with the nurse in charge that she will be 15 to 30 minutes late. There is only a 30-minute overlap between your timetables to handover to your colleague. You need to leave on time as you have a social engagement to attend with your partner.

Rank the following actions in response to this situation in ascending order of appropriateness:

A. Make a list of the patients under your care on the AAU, detailing their outstanding issues, leaving this on the doctor's office notice board when your shift ends and then leave at the end of your shift.
B. Quickly go around each of the patients on the AAU, leaving an entry in the notes highlighting the major outstanding issues relating to each patient and then leave at the end of your shift.
C. Make a list of patients and outstanding investigations to give to your colleague as soon as she arrives.
D. Ask your registrar if you can leave a list of your patients and their outstanding issues with him to give to your colleague when she arrives and then leave at the end of your shift.
E. Leave a message for your partner explaining that you will be 30 minutes late.

This question gives you the opportunity to demonstrate a conscientious attitude by prioritising patient care over personal concerns and team working. It would be unfair on your colleague to not give them the opportunity to ask any questions about the handover. The safest option is (E) as it ensures a comprehensive handover and doesn't sacrifice patient safety. The other options all involve a non-verbal handover which risks patient safety.

If you weren't given these options, you could instead talk the interviewer through your reasoning:
"So to summarise, I am faced with the situation where I am finishing my shift and the doctor taking over is running late. If I overstay, I will be late for my social commitment. If I leave, the handover will be inefficient and important information relevant to patient care may not get passed on.

In this situation, I have the option to write all the remaining tasks on paper and either give them to another person that is coming in to pass on to the next person or leave it in an office for the attention of the incoming doctor. Whilst this may be reasonable, it's not the best as there is a risk that the information may not get passed on at all or not in a timely manner which could compromise patient care.

I feel the best option would be for me to call my partner to let them know that I will be running late and wait for the incoming doctor to do a face-to-face handover"

Many applicants find the Mnemonic *INSIST* helpful when structuring their answers:

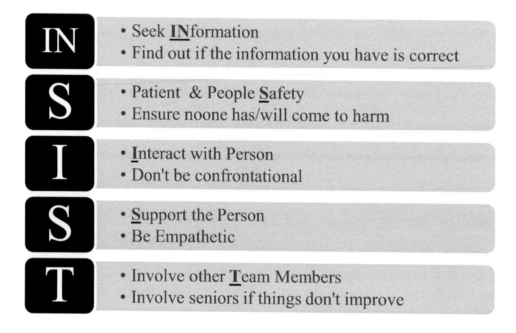

IN
- Seek **IN**formation
- Find out if the information you have is correct

S
- Patient & People **S**afety
- Ensure noone has/will come to harm

I
- **I**nteract with Person
- Don't be confrontational

S
- **S**upport the Person
- Be Empathetic

T
- Involve other **T**eam Members
- Involve seniors if things don't improve

We now turn to an example Station 3 interview that picks up immediately following the ethical scenario. We then discuss more specific examples of scenarios that are likely to appear during Station 3. We cover the main principles required to answer them successfully, and give advice on what not to include in these answers.

Example Professionalism Interview

Interviewer: *Thank you for your responses to our ethical scenario. Now we are going turn and ask you about a different scenario.*

Candidate: *Of course.*

Interviewer: *You are the IM Stage 1 doctor on call on night shifts, and are on the admission clerking team. You have arrived for evening handover, and you have been informed that your registrar has called in sick and is not going to be in work. You are told that it is looking really busy in A&E, and there are many sick medical patients waiting to be seen. Please talk us through the situation, including what is going on in your mind, and tell us what you would do next.*

Candidate: *Thank you. That certainly sounds like a challenging situation. I will just take a brief moment to gather my thoughts about how I would tackle this situation.*

Interviewer: *No problem, take your time.*

Candidate: *My first concern is that of patient safety: and to me, I see a couple of places where this could be compromised in this case.*

Firstly, there is the concern that I would be leading a busy acute medical take, which I am not yet fully qualified to do. I would also be doing this without a senior doctor, and so would be concerned I couldn't ask questions of a senior when there are things I am unsure of.

Secondly, I am worried that there are a significant number of patients waiting, and so they need to be seen as quickly as possible. Therefore, I would try to make arrangements as soon as possible at the start of my shift, but would need to ensure that this doesn't delay me significantly from starting to see the patients in order to avoid harm coming to them.

As such, I would like to ask a couple of questions to ensure I have a proper grasp on the situation.

Interviewer: *Please do.*

Candidate: *I would like to know if the registrar that called in sick is the only medical registrar in the hospital, or if there is another that is, for example, responsible for wards. If there was then I would get in touch with them as soon as possible to ask for their advice and make them aware of the risks to patient safety. I would also like to know if there is any other doctor on my team.*

Interviewer: *There is no second medical registrar available unfortunately. You also have an FY1 colleague working on the shift with you.*

Candidate: *Due to the risk to patient safety, I feel therefore that I should make the on call medical consultant aware of the situation.*

Interviewer: *OK, how would you do that?*

Candidate: *I would contact the consultant through switchboard, and explain the situation along with my concerns to them, and ask them what they would advise at this stage.*

Interviewer: *They explain that they are happy for you to call them if you are concerned with any case that you see, and that if the number of medical patients waiting to be seen continues to increase despite your best efforts then you should contact them again and they can come in to hospital.*

Candidate: *I understand. Whilst I may have preferred their assistance from the start of the shift, my concerns for patient safety now switch to the fact that there are several sick patients that need to be seen as a matter of urgency. I would therefore commence seeing these patients, keeping a low threshold to return the call to the consultant if either of the above circumstances were to arise.*

Interviewer: *Is there anything else you could do to ensure the operation runs as smoothly as possible?*

Candidate: *I would ensure that I had regular meetings with my FY1 colleague. I would explain the situation to them and explain that we may have a challenging night ahead but that our first concern was for the safety of the patients we would be seeing. Together, we would work out an appropriate action plan that would allow me to distribute some work to the FY1 to improve the efficiency with which I could see new patients.*

Interviewer: *Is there anything you could do to try to prevent this from happening again?*

Candidate: *Following the shift, I would get in touch with my educational supervisor and the consultant in charge of the acute medical unit. I would explain the situation to them and ask them to confirm what the plan should be in these situations. If there was no official protocol in place, I would ask if we could draw one up such that there is a specific plan in place if this were to happen again.*

Interviewer: *Thank you for your answers.*

Candidate: *Thank you for your time.*

Analysis:

This situation is clearly an uncomfortable one for any junior doctor to be in: the lack of appropriate and experienced senior advice is always concerning. In addition, the team is down a doctor, which will have an impact on the workload of each doctor and the ability of the team to see new patients.

The candidate correctly and quickly identifies that there are risks to **patient safety** in this case. The candidate explains what they think those risks are, and then tries to solve the problem in an efficient way. They show to the interviewers that they understand the hierarchy in place, and know to follow that during a situation such as this. They also demonstrate a willingness to step up to the plate to do their best to ensure patient safety is not compromised when the consultant explains they wouldn't come in straight away.

The interviewers will be impressed in this scenario with candidates who show that they are well-versed in dealing with situations that put them outside of their comfort zone. They want to see that future IM trainees know what to do in challenging professional situations, and that they retain the core focus on patient safety throughout.

We will now move onto a discussion of specific professionalism scenarios that may come up during the interview.

Example Professionalism Scenarios

1) You are a junior doctor on cardiology. Your consultant in charge turns up on Monday morning smelling strongly of alcohol. What do you do?

This question tests your ability to deal with a senior colleague whom you suspect is drinking alcohol and has turned up to work smelling of alcohol. There is usually a pattern to follow when answering these questions: try to approach the person in question to gather a bit of information: are they, in fact, drinking alcohol? You may have been mistaken and it would, therefore, be wrong to take any further action. Next, you should try and explore the reason behind their behaviour: is it a transient and short-lasting event that has caused the consultant to drink? If so, hopefully there shouldn't be a long-term issue here. Thirdly, the interviewer would like to hear that you are taking steps to ensure that patients are safe. This may involve asking the consultant politely to get some rest and go home: clinical errors or prescribing errors due to alcohol consumption could potentially be deadly. They will want to know what you would do if the consultant declined. Lastly, you may want to suggest the consultant seek some help.

A Bad Response:
Smelling strongly of alcohol at your workplace is, in my opinion, unacceptable. The consultant, although a senior figure, should know better and I think his behaviour should be reported promptly. The consequences of having a drunken consultant in the clinical area are unsafe and it also tarnishes the doctors' reputation as a whole. I would therefore ask my registrar to have a word with the consultant and hopefully, the matter will be escalated to the medical director who can then decide the best course of action.

Response Analysis:
This candidate is rather rash in his/her approach to the situation. Firstly, there is only a suspicion that the consultant is drinking alcohol. It is thus better to sensitively explore this first before discussing the situation with anybody else. Reporting somebody without first getting the facts straight is inappropriate. Whilst you can seek help from your registrar who will be senior to you, the answer here sounds more like you are passing the buck to the registrar and asking them to sort the situation out rather than seeking advice and acting on the advice yourself; interviewers will appreciate you being proactive and sorting matters out yourself.

A Good Response:
This is a complex scenario. As there is only a presumption here that the consultant has been drinking (he smells of alcohol only), I would approach him and politely ask him if he has been drinking any alcohol. I would next offer to explore his behaviour by asking him what has led him to drink alcohol and what has led him to still smell of it when he comes into work. I would then suggest he takes the rest of the day off after ensuring his shift is covered by explaining that patient safety may be compromised if he practices medicine under the influence. If he refused to do this, I would contact my educational supervisor for urgent advice. Lastly, I would suggest to him that he seeks further help, either by going to his GP or going to occupational health.

Response Analysis:
This answer takes a calm and measured approach to the situation by following the 'usual' steps for this type of scenario. The candidate is information gathering rather than reporting the consultant straight away. There is also an awareness that patient safety may be at risk, and the candidate provides a solution to tackle this and understands the need to be sensitive here.

Overall:
Professionalism questions such as this can be difficult, and the key is to take a measured and calm approach to the situation. Reporting individuals straight away before attempting to resolve the situation between teams is often not the right approach, and interviewers would rather you to talk to the person in question yourself and take it from there. But remember that patient safety is the most important aspect here and if the consultant were to refuse to go home and continue seeing patients under the influence, you may then need to escalate the situation to someone more senior to you to ensure that patients are not in danger.

2) You're on a busy on call admission shift with your registrar who tells you that he feels 'fed up and just wants to end it all'. You know he has gone through a difficult divorce and is on anti-depressants. What would you do?

This question aims to assess your ability to take the correct steps to effectively deal with a complex scenario. Approach this situation like the other professionalism questions in this book: discuss the person in question's feelings, ensure patient safety is maintained, and advise the person to seek help.

A Bad Response:

This is a rather tricky question. I'm not sure exactly what I would do: perhaps I would like to ask my fellow colleagues what they would do if they were in my shoes. I am quite concerned that the registrar wants to 'end it all', but it is a busy shift. I think he should have called in sick if he didn't feel like working today. I could speak to the consultant about him because he is in charge and, therefore, should be able to deal with the situation effectively. Or perhaps his medication has not been titrated enough? Maybe I can advise him to increase the dose of his medication and see if that makes him feel better?

Response Analysis:

It is important to support your colleagues through difficult times and act compassionate towards them, just like you would with any patient. Therefore, try to listen to them and help them out rather than worry about how busy A+E is. Whilst asking fellow colleagues for advice is good practice, it may be that the registrar has come to you in confidence and would not want you to discuss his situation with others. Also, remember that it is better for you to suggest for the registrar to raise the issue with their consultant rather than you raising it. The registrar will be in a much better position to explain his/her situation than you will. It is dangerous to ask him to increase the dose of his medication - this should be left to the person who prescribes the medication, as they will have information about his other medical conditions and know if it is indeed safe to increase the dose. In this way, it may have been more appropriate to ask the registrar to seek help from his/her own doctor.

A Good Response:

This is a difficult situation but this is how I would approach it. I would firstly suggest to the registrar to move to a quieter room to explore his feelings further. Before doing this, I would ensure there is adequate staff cover and inform the nurses of our temporary absence on the ward. I would assess whether I felt the patient's low mood meant that he was a risk to patient safety, and if so would advise he took the rest of the shift off. From the scenario, it seems as if his low mood is poorly controlled on the current medication and I would, therefore, advise him to book an appointment to see his GP. Furthermore, I would advise him to discuss his issues and concerns with his educational supervisor, as they will be experienced in dealing with pastoral care issues.

Response Analysis:

This answer demonstrates a good understanding of the necessary steps to deal with a complex scenario. It shows that it is important to discuss the registrar's feelings with him, not only to provide colleague support, but also to understand how severe the low mood is in order to establish whether he is able to continue with work and not compromise patient safety. It also nicely highlights that communicating with the nurse and ensuring the shift is covered is very important. The answer also provides longer-term management options and offers the registrar further advice on who to turn to for further help.

Overall:

Try not to discuss sensitive issues with your peers (so spreading 'gossip') but rather try and discuss it with the person in question directly. If you cannot find a solution, then ask him/her to escalate the situation to the consultant in charge. Remember, patient safety is critical important here and if the registrar is too depressed to work, he/she will need to step out of the clinical area. Lastly, remember there are a number of people in the hospital that are trained to help doctors with these types of issues.

3) You are faced with a patient's angry relatives. The patient is sleeping poorly and complains that the ward staff are ignoring her. She is very tearful. What do you do?

Sometimes hospitals can fail in their care and complaints are made. This is becoming increasingly common, and is a normal part of working in the NHS. Lack of time and attention paid to patients means that serious mistakes can be made. Medical staff may not have enough time with each individual patient, and so their full medical and emotional needs may not be met. Patients can be left in a high state of anxiety because staff don't have time to talk to them enough.

It is important to take a holistic approach to patient management (consider the whole person, meaning their physical, emotional, mental, and spiritual health).

The key skill needed for dealing with angry patients or relatives is communication, but you must do so in a professional manner, and therefore this type of scenario can also appear in the professionalism interview.

A Bad Response:
1) I would apologise profusely and make time to spend with the patient.

2) I can understand why the relatives were angry. However, I would explain that the staff are very busy at the moment, and that they will assist the patient as soon as they were available.

Response Analysis:
In the first answer, the candidate misses the complex nature of the situation by simply stating they would 'make time'. As you will have no doubt experienced already, carving out time is not easy. The second answer is almost the opposite. It is likely to anger the relatives. The lack of apology and the rush to defend the service gives an impression of lack of empathy. Empathy is an essential quality in a doctor and it is important to acknowledge and address the relatives' concerns.

A Good Response:
Good communication skills are key to fulfilling a doctor's role. This includes listening. I would first apologise and then listen to the relatives concerns, trying to find out more about the situation – is the patient more concerned about the lack of attention or the reduced sleep? I would then work with the relatives and patient to address the patient's primary concern – partnership between healthcare professionals and patients is important in order to produce a patient centred culture in the NHS.

Response Analysis:
This answer has a better structure. It begins by very quickly getting to the point of the question – interviewers want to know about your communication skills. By acknowledging this early, the interviewers know you are aware of the key issue in this question. The candidate also shows a caring and reflective nature by realising that there may be more than one reason for the patient's emotional state (*'is the patient more concerned about the lack of attention or the reduced sleep?'*). Using the phrase *'partnership between healthcare professionals and patients'* shows the candidate is aware of the need for joint decision making between the patient and doctor, which is a cornerstone of good communication skills.

Overall:
A good answer will show empathy and showcase your communication skills. It is important to remember that healthcare professionals work together with patients to deliver optimum care.

4) You are just about to finish your work for the day when the ward nurse asks you to talk to the angry sister of a patient who is admitted under a different team. You have a dinner date with your partner and need to drive to the restaurant. What would you do?

This question is about dealing with an angry relative as well as balancing work and social plans. It also tests your time and people management skills. Your response to stress will also be assessed. If you don't leave in time, you will be late. Do you get stressed in this situation?

A Bad Response:

I would say to the nurse that I had finished for the day and as this was not my patient anyway that she should call someone else to speak with the relative.

Response Analysis:

The trainee comes across as someone who shirks from responsibility and has a lack of empathy. They fail to actually find out what the problem is from the nurse. This is important because simple issues can be quickly resolved, e.g. analgesia if the brother was in lots of pain. This would mean that the ward nurse wouldn't be left with an angry relative. Although it's important that you take your breaks as a doctor and leave on time, it's also important not to neglect your duties.

A Good Response:

This patient is not on my team but is being managed by Dr Smith's team. What is the problem anyway? If it is something quick maybe I could talk to the relative, and if it requires more discussion I'd advise her to make an appointment to see Dr Smith who is the responsible consultant. I can also bleep someone in Dr Smith's team so that they can explain this to the sister. If this is clinically urgent, I am happy to stay behind but I'll need to make a quick call to my fiancée to explain that I'll be late.

Response Analysis:

Answering this way, you have demonstrated that you are a hard-working doctor that will work well in a team, does not get stressed with unexpected situations, empathise well, and are able to take extra steps to ensure your patients' welfare is maintained at all times. It shows that you know what would be required in similar circumstances where leaving early may put patient safety at risk.

Overall:

You will no doubt have already come across this type of situation in your life as a doctor. In such scenarios, it is useful to ensure that your actions don't compromise patient safety (in life and death situations you can't walk away). If someone wants to know about the progress of the family member, you should be able to spend a few minutes (if it is a quick discussion) to diffuse the situation and offer to get someone else from the parent team to have an in-depth discussion. In some ways, it is irrelevant that the patient is from a different team as the on-call doctor is also likely not to be from the same team.

5) What is clinical governance? Why is it important?

Clinical governance refers to the systematic approach used by NHS Trusts to maintain and improve the quality of patient care within the health service. Prior to the introduction of clinical governance, NHS Trusts were responsible only for the financial management of their organisation and it was the responsibility of individual health care professionals to maintain high standards of care. Nowadays, each trust (alongside the individual clinicians) is responsible for maintaining the highest possible standard of care and doing so in the safest possible manner. The best answers to this question will demonstrate how effective clinical governance is achieved and in doing so will explain its importance.

A Bad Response:

Clinical governance is the process by which NHS Trusts ensure that their health care provision is delivered in the most efficient way. In a time when cuts to healthcare budgets are commonplace, trusts have to find new ways to cut spending while still providing an appropriate level of care. The cornerstone of clinical governance is finding the most cost-effective methods to serve the local population.

Response Analysis:

This answer shows a lack of understanding of clinical governance. Clinical governance refers only to the process by which trusts ensure the highest standard of clinical care. Cost-effectiveness of treatments may form part of clinical governance but financial factors are not the focus of clinical governance. It should be noted that trusts are under increasing pressure to control spending but this is not the same as clinical governance.

A Good Response:

Clinical governance is the systematic approach used by NHS Trusts to maintain and improve the quality of patient care within the health service. It comprises several different components. The trust and clinicians are together responsible for continued professional development so that all professional knowledge is up to date. The trust must commit to clinical audit/quality improvement in which clinical practice is reviewed, altered and reassessed, and also to make decisions surrounding clinical practice based on clinical effectiveness. Effectiveness can take into consideration things like value for money and QALYs. Trusts also commit to evidence-based medicine and to find ways to introduce new research into practice in a way that reduces the lag between new discoveries and a reduction in associated morbidities.

In order to ensure proper clinical governance is possible, trusts commit to collect high-quality data on their processes and to allow this data to be openly scrutinised in order that bad practice cannot continue unnoticed.

Ultimately, clinical governance is important in creating systems in which bad practice is stamped out and excellent practice is able to flourish.

Response Analysis:

This is a very thorough answer that explains the mechanisms by which clinical governance is achieved. Crucially, this answer demonstrates an understanding that every mechanism is put in place with the main priority of achieving the highest standard of clinical care.

Overall:

To summarise, clinical governance is about the NHS trust taking appropriate steps to provide the 'right care to the right patients, at the right time, by the right people in the right place'. This is done by ensuring that staff remain up-to-date, perform regular audits and quality improvement projects, implement evidence-based medicine, and have sufficient opportunity to learn from mistakes.

6) You are a junior doctor and on your way back from work after a busy night shift. At the car park, you find someone who has collapsed and requires CPR. You remember that you aren't insured to do CPR outside the hospital – what do you do?

This is a potentially tricky question and some background reading into the laws that govern the application of healthcare in the UK would, of course, be desirable. However, most interviewers will not expect you to be familiar with the intricacies of the law and so will simply be looking for good reasoning ability. You should approach this question systematically. An example of such a systematic approach is the following: Firstly, does the junior doctor have a duty of care to this member of the public? Secondly, what standard of care is expected of them? Thirdly, can they be held to account for increasing the harm to the member of the public?

A Bad Response:

No, because if something goes wrong then the person's family may sue the junior doctor. Additionally, the collapsed person isn't the doctor's patient and so they have no responsibility for them.

Response Analysis:

Several issues arise with this answer. Firstly, the law states that they will only be liable for damages if their action leaves the recipient in a worse position than if no action at all had been taken. Given that the person would have almost certainly died without CPR, it seems that the junior doctor would be justified in administering CPR without fear of liability. Secondly, the candidate states that the doctor has no duty of care because the person is not their patient. This may be true; however, the interviewers would begin to severely question this individual's morality if they were to not apply their potentially lifesaving skills in this situation simply because they did not have a formal duty of care. Remember that even as a member of public, it is crucial to raise an alarm, seek assistance to ensure that the patient gets the treatment.

A Good Response:

I'm not entirely sure of the finer points of the law, however, I believe that I should provide CPR in this scenario. This is mainly from a moral point of view due to a doctor having the knowledge to potentially save this person's life. Doctors can administer treatments without consent if the individual is unable to give consent and it is deemed to be in the patient's best interests. Both these conditions seem to apply here.

I would only recommend doing so as long as the doctor felt they were able to provide CPR to the level expected (and was not off duty and under the influence of alcohol, for example), as this could cause a serious risk to patient safety. Even if they are not able to provide CPR, they should raise alarm to get help by calling 999.

Response Analysis:

The candidate does well to present a good, logical argument with a nice conclusion at the end. Importantly, they admit to the interviewer that they are not an expert on the law but show how the small bits they do know (when treatment without explicit consent is appropriate) may be applied to this situation. The candidate even touches upon counter-arguments, e.g. what if the doctor is incapacitated for some reason (the candidate suggests a situation whereby the off-duty doctor may be under the influence of alcohol).

Overall:

This is a typical question where the interviewer is unlikely to expect you to know exactly what the law is. However, they want to see how you think your way through tricky problems. They may well drip-feed you pieces of information to see how you think on your feet and how you can adapt your argument as new information comes to light. Plenty of practice in thinking about these sorts of dilemmas will make you more comfortable with these questions.

Finally, once again it is important to consider patient safety: patient safety is clearly at risk if the CPR is not performed (and the law backs this up). However (and the second candidate covers this), it is important that you only act when you are able to provide the standard of care that you are expected to provide (i.e. not when under the influence of alcohol), as doing so could create a significant risk to patient safety.

FINAL ADVICE

Congratulations for making the decision to apply to Internal Medicine Stage 1: this is the start of an extremely exciting phase in any aspiring physician's career. You should view the application with anticipation and enthusiasm and ensure this comes across in your application and interview. Interviewers are looking for their future registrars and colleagues, and seeing a bright face, excited about their future in medicine, always improves their thinking about the candidate.

Make sure you complete each and every section of the application to the best of your ability, and think about your physical portfolio at the same time as this will help immensely with the preparation of your portfolio.

It is important to ensure that you spend enough time preparing for the interview – practice interviews are the key! – such that you are no longer unsure of what to expect on the day and what sorts of things you will be asked. Be up to date with the underlying medical knowledge required, but know that there is always an important structure to fall back on that will see you through the scenarios.

We hope that the guidance and information provided throughout this book will make you feel much more confident as the interview approaches, and most importantly will let your true enthusiasm shine through.

Good luck!

Dr Charles Earnshaw and Dr Rohan Agarwal

Acknowledgements

Charles Earnshaw is funded by a National Institute for Health Research Academic Clinical Fellowship.

About Us

Infinity Books is the publishing division of *Infinity Education*. We currently publish over 85 titles across a range of subject areas – covering specialised admissions tests, examination techniques, personal statement guides, plus everything else you need to improve your chances of getting on to competitive courses such as medicine and law, as well as into universities such as Oxford and Cambridge.

Outside of publishing we also operate a highly successful tuition division, called UniAdmissions. This company was founded in 2013 by Dr Rohan Agarwal and Dr David Salt, both Cambridge Medical graduates with several years of tutoring experience. Since then, every year, hundreds of applicants and schools work with us on our programmes. Through the programmes we offer, we deliver expert tuition, exclusive course places, online courses, best-selling textbooks and much more.

With a team of over 1,000 Oxbridge tutors and a proven track record, UniAdmissions have quickly become the UK's number one admissions company.

Visit and engage with us at:

Website (UniAdmissions): www.uniadmissions.co.uk

Facebook: www.facebook.com/uniadmissionsuk

YOUR FREE BOOK

Thanks for purchasing this Ultimate Book. Readers like you have the power to make or break a book –hopefully you found this one useful and informative. *The Oxbridge Medical Society* would love to hear about your experiences with this book. As thanks for your time we'll send you another ebook from our Ultimate Guide series absolutely <u>FREE</u>!

How to Redeem Your Free Ebook

1) Find the book you have on your Amazon
purchase history or your email receipt to help find the book on Amazon.

2) On the product page at the Customer Reviews area, click 'Write a customer review'. Write your review and post it! Copy the review page or take a screen shot of the review you have left.

3) Head over to www.uniadmissions.co.uk/oxbridge-free-book and select your chosen free ebook!

Your ebook will then be emailed to you – it's as simple as that!

Printed in Great Britain
by Amazon

16137091R00086